The Little Road

The Story of the
Macomb Industry & Littleton Railway

By Frank G. Hicks

WESTERN ILLINOIS UNIVERSITY
MACOMB, ILLINOIS

Copyright © 2006 by Western Illinois University

This book is printed on acid-free paper.

Western Illinois University Libraries
Western Illinois University College of Arts and Sciences
Macomb, Illinois 61455

Printed and bound in the United States of America

ISBN: 0-9777116-0-9

Front cover photo: Macomb & Western Illinois locomotive number 2 is "on the point" of a southbound mixed train consisting of a CB&Q boxcar and M&WI coach number 2 at Industry sometime during 1905 or 1906.
Title page: This early view of the M&WI Industry depot faces northwest and shows the siding just north of the depot.
Back cover photo: One of the original M&WI stock certificates, this is #19. The blank lines denoting ownership and transfer date indicate that, like the rest of the M&WI's stock, the Bank of Macomb was never able to sell this share.

All three images are from Western Illinois University (WIU) Archives and Special Collections Unit.

The editors wish to thank the Haines Family Fund for Regional Studies for assisting with the publication of this inaugural volume of the New Western Illinois University Monograph Series.

THE NEW WESTERN ILLINOIS MONOGRAPH SERIES
Jeffrey Hancks and Susan Martinelli-Fernandez, Series Editors

Series Editorial Board:
Martin Dupuis
Raymond Greene
Greg Hall
John E. Hallwas
Inessa Levi (Ex-officio)
Jeffrey Matlak
Polly F. Radosh
David Stevenson

THE WESTERN ILLINOIS MONOGRAPH SERIES

Susan Glaspell: Voice From the Heartland (1983)
Marcia Noe

Thomas Gregg: Early Illinois Journalist (1983)
John E. Hallwas

John Hay's Pike County: Two Tales and Seven Ballads (1984)
Edited with an Introduction by George Monteiro

Robert G. Ingersoll: Peoria's Pagan Politician (1984)
Mark A. Plummer

Joseph Smith, Jr.'s Red Brick Store (1985)
Roger D. Launius and F. Mark McKiernan

We Are Sherman's Men: The Civil War Letters of Henry Orendorff (1986)
William M. Anderson

Adelaide Johnson: To Make Immortal Their Adventurous Will (1986)
Shirley J. Burton

Lincoln's Springfield in the Civil War (1991)
Camilla A. Quinn

The New Western Illinois Monograph Series is published by the University Libraries and the College of Arts and Sciences at Western Illinois University. The series supports studies in the biography, history, geography, ethnography, literature, politics, and culture of the western Illinois region. Correspondence about the original Western Illinois Monograph Series or manuscripts for the new series should be sent to Professor Susan Martinelli-Fernandez, College of Arts and Sciences, Western Illinois University, Macomb, Illinois 61455.

Series Acknowledgements

This is the first volume of the *New Western Illinois Monograph Series*. The original monograph series produced eight outstanding volumes in the 1980s and the early 1990s, but unfortunately it did not survive a previous budget cut. It was not the original intent of WIU to reinstate the series, but after discussions with Distinguished Professor Emeritus John Hallwas and former Dean of Libraries James Huesmann, the timing seemed right to pursue it. My position of Endowed Professor of Icarian and Regional Studies was created in July 2005, and one of my primary duties is to promote the region's history and culture. Furthermore, the University Libraries has been successful in raising external funds to promote regional studies, establishing a budget from which this book was partially produced. With the help of College of Arts and Sciences Dean Inessa Levi, a new series editorial board has been formed, drawing from the extraordinary faculty of the Western Illinois University Libraries and the College of Arts and Sciences. We envision publishing one book each year on topics related to western Illinois regional studies. As this book was already well underway before the new editorial board was created, this volume did not pass through the members' hands. Thus, any mistakes in the editorial process rest solely with me.

Most of the thanks for this volume go to 2005 WIU graduate Frank Hicks. Frank worked tirelessly on this manuscript on his own time for several years. His goal was to simply donate his research notes and papers to the Archives. However, it was immediately apparent to us in the Archives that his tremendous work needed to be shared with a wider audience. Frank's passion for railroads brought him to the WIU Archives; the outstanding service he received from the staff and his dedication to the project kept him coming back. The end result is a phenomenal contribution to western Illinois regional studies. Archives staff members William Cook and Kathy Nichols provided invaluable assistance throughout the research process. Marla Vizdal volunteered graciously to edit the manuscript, and she worked diligently with several campus offices to get the book printed. Countless other persons on the WIU campus provided support to create this book. They remain anonymous, but their work is greatly appreciated.

On behalf of the series editorial board, we look forward to producing additional monographs and sharing our interest in western Illinois regional studies.

Jeffrey Hancks
Endowed Professor of Icarian and Regional Studies
Western Illinois University

Foreword

Macomb, Illinois was very different at the dawn of the 20th century than it is now. Like all of the cities in McDonough County it was a farm town, just another county seat along the line of the Chicago Burlington & Quincy Railroad. But early in the new century the city began to change. Ultimately the most significant change would be the establishment of the Western Illinois State Normal School. But there was another change at the dawn of the century that signaled the advancement of Macomb: it got its own railroad.

The Macomb Industry & Littleton Railway, or MI&L, ran south out of Macomb twenty miles, serving the communities of Industry and Littleton and the farmers in between. Its trains ran through McDonough and Schuyler Counties for more than a quarter of a century, carrying people and products affordably, and generally reliably, to what had only fifty years before been the frontier of the United States. Farmers shipped out livestock and grain destined for the Chicago markets; merchants shipped in goods to sell in their stores; customers shipped in products ordered from remote locations; and everyone rode the train. The MI&L was affectionately nicknamed the "Little Road" by the local newspapers. Unlike the massive, impersonal Burlington system that ran through Macomb, the MI&L was owned and operated by locals. The train would stop at any house or corner along its route to pick someone up or let someone off. All that was required for front door delivery was a quick request of the engineer, and when the train arrived, the crew would obligingly unload the merchandise before continuing on their way. The conductors and engineers knew everyone who lived along the route, and everyone knew them. Personal service was a way of doing business.

The story of the MI&L is a twisting, tortured one, for from a purely financial perspective the railroad probably should never have been built. It was the product of the optimistic interurban boom of the early 20th century and the determination of its owners to benefit their communities even if it meant running a money losing operation. Though never very profitable, in the end it did benefit the people and towns it served and for decades was an accepted and important part of life for thousands of people. This is the story of the Macomb Industry & Littleton Railway – "The Little Road."

Acknowledgements

First and foremost, I would like to thank Bill Cook, Kathy Nichols and Marla Vizdal of Western Illinois University's Archives and Special Collections Unit. For a year and a half they put up with my incessant demands on their time and patience, and without their help not a single page of this history would have been possible. Thanks go to Joe Piersen of the Chicago & North Western Historical Society, Fred Ash, Bob Watson, and Dr. Harold Cox for their help in tracing roster information. I would also like to thank the volunteers of the Schuyler County Jail Museum for their assistance and Viletta Hilary for her time and reminiscences. Randall Hicks and Dave Swanson were kind enough to proofread draft copies of this work and provided valuable insight. Jeff Hancks provided valuable assistance with publication work.

This book is dedicated to my father, to whom I owe my lifelong interest in trains.

Table of Contents

Series Description	*iii*
Series Acknowledgements	*iv*
Foreword	*v*
Acknowledgements	*vi*
Map of The Little Road's Stations	viii
1. The Coming of the Railroad	1
2. The Electric Road	11
3. In the Balance	25
4. Men of Industry	35
5. Strides of Progress	45
Afterword	57
Appendix A - Trackage and Structures	59
Appendix B - Rolling Stock	67
Appendix C - MI&L Annual Reports	73
End Notes	77
Bibliography	85

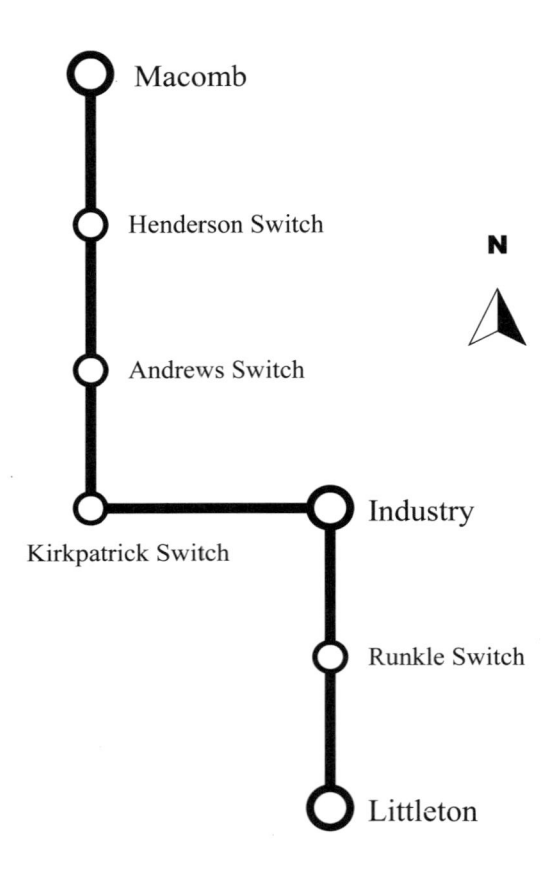

A simple diagram of the MI&L route showing timetable locations. Detailed track maps can be found in Appendix A.

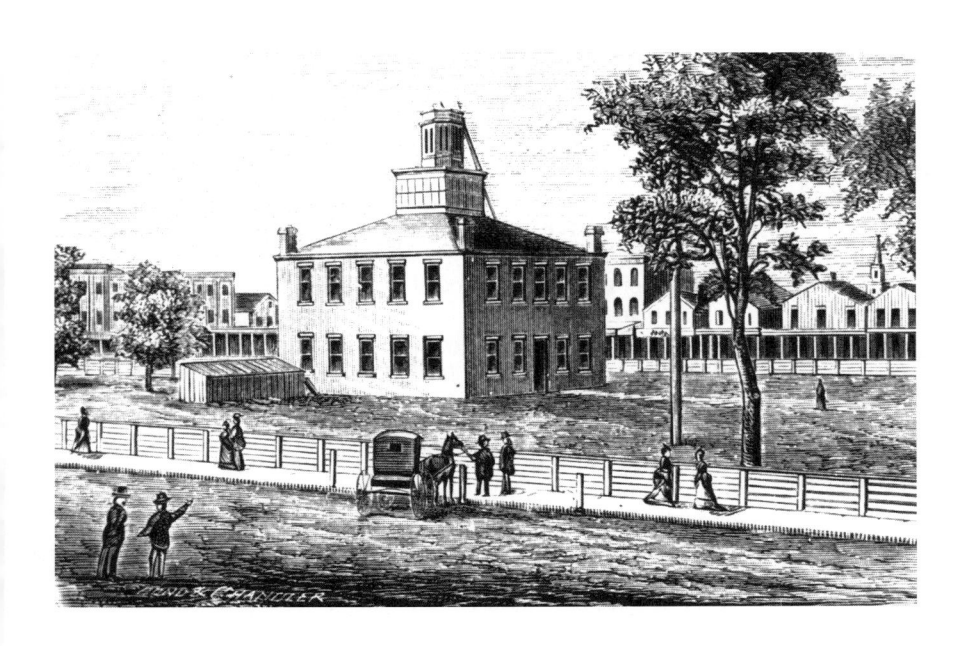

The Coming of the Railroad

The history of the Macomb Industry & Littleton Railway runs hand-in-hand with the history of Macomb and the areas surrounding it, and that story begins long before the first white settlers even arrived in modern McDonough County. The earliest French explorers first saw Illinois when they traversed the Mississippi and Illinois rivers in the late 1600s; a few settlements followed and in 1717 the region was made part of the Louisiana Territory. It became British land in 1763 after the French and Indian War, and fifteen years later George Rogers Clark captured Kaskaskia and Cahokia and claimed the land for the state of Virginia. In 1784 Virginia ceded Illinois County, as it was called, to the United States federal government. At first it was part of the Northwest Territory, then in 1800 the Indiana Territory was formed with boundaries encompassing modern Illinois. In 1809 the Illinois Territory was created, and nine years later Illinois became a state and its modern boundaries were established.[1]

When Illinois became a state, there were about 40,000 whites living within its borders, though not a single one of them in modern McDonough County. Much of west-central Illinois, including the area around Macomb, was part of the Military Tract. This was land that had been set aside for soldiers who had served in the War of 1812, in increments of 160-320 acres per

The above drawing shows the original courthouse in Macomb as it appeared during the 1830s, soon after it was built. Bateman & Shelby, <u>The Historical Encyclopedia of Illinois and McDonough County</u>.

man. Many soldiers never claimed their land, and only a handful ever moved to western Illinois. The first white settlers in McDonough County arrived in 1826, around the time the county was separated from Pike County, its borders fixed, and its governance put under the control of Schuyler County. The first settlement was about a mile southeast of where Industry was later founded, and over the next four years more settlements sprang up near the current locations of Blandinsville and Macomb. In 1830 McDonough County was officially founded and the settlement of Washington, changed to Macomb later in the year, at its center, was made the county seat. The county was named for Commodore Thomas MacDonough, who had commanded the victorious American fleet against the British in the Battle of Lake Champlain in 1814, while the county seat was named for General Alexander Macomb, commander of the American land forces at Plattsburg in that same battle.[2]

Macomb expanded steadily in the years after the county was created. In 1841 it was incorporated as a village; fifteen years later it was incorporated as a city. McDonough County grew up around it as well, with settlements in the south, closer to Schuyler County and the Illinois River, being established earlier than in the north. One of the first of these was Industry.[3]

The first settler on the current site of Industry was a blacksmith who set up shop in 1846. At the time there were virtually no real towns in the surrounding countryside; even the nearest post office was fairly isolated. Not until 1850 did other businesses begin to cluster around the lone blacksmith shop, but the settlement began growing, and in 1855 the town, by now known as Industry, was laid out and surveyed. It wasn't until two years later that the current political townships in McDonough County were established, with Industry Township encompassing the area around the new settlement. In 1867 the town of Industry was officially incorporated, and in the following years Industry prospered as the largest town for ten miles in any direction.[4]

Six miles south of Industry lay the town of Littleton, over the border in Schuyler County. The first white settlers in Schuyler County arrived in the Rushville area in 1823, and only two years later the county was officially created. What was later known as Littleton Township was originally Oregon Township. The first settlers in the area arrived in the northern part of the township in 1836 and laid out the town of Doddsville, right on the border with McDonough County. Thirteen years later James Little settled in the exact center of the township and laid out a new town, Littleton. The village expanded quickly, surviving a tornado that destroyed much of the town in 1856, and growing to a size of more than 1,000 by the end of the century.[5]

The most important development in Macomb's first century of existence was the coming of the railroad. The first successful steam locomotives had been developed in England in the late 1820s and the technology had quickly spread across the Atlantic. A few short railroads were built on the east coast in the early 1830s, and by the 1840s they had been greatly extended and expanded. By 1840 it was becoming clear that railroads were the best way to connect the far corners of the United States, and railroad lines began to be built as far west as the Mississippi Valley. A network of railroads criss-crossing the state of Illinois was conceived as early as the late 1830s. By 1850 the first railroads were built west out of Chicago as far as Elgin and Aurora. Within the next year or so canvassers, or fundraisers, spread out across the state to raise interest in, and money for, the railroads that would be built to the Mississippi and beyond.[6]

One of these planned railroad lines was the Northern Cross Railroad, renamed the Quincy & Chicago Railroad in 1857. The Northern Cross would be built between Quincy in the south and Galesburg in the north. It would connect with the Central Military Tract Railroad and the Aurora Branch Railroad being constructed between Galesburg and Chicago, thereby linking western Illinois with the largest city in the state, as well as with Lake Michigan. The intended route went straight through McDonough County and, of course, through Macomb.[7]

The Northern Cross, the second railroad in Illinois to bear the name, was originally conceived in early 1851 as a link between the Mississippi River at Quincy, and the Illinois & Michigan Canal. At the same time, though, there were two other railroads extending toward each other from Galesburg and Chicago: the Aurora Branch Railroad, renamed the Chicago & Aurora Railroad in 1852, building southwest from Chicago, and the Central Military Tract Railroad, building northeast from Galesburg. The Chicago & Aurora Railroad and the Central Military Tract Railroad managements were able to persuade the Northern Cross to change its northern terminus to Galesburg, thereby paving the way for the creation of a through route from Chicago to Quincy.[8]

The first railroad meeting in Macomb was on November 5, 1851. It was then that the Northern Cross' management presented their proposal for the railroad from Quincy to Galesburg, and asked for McDonough County to purchase $50,000 worth of stock in the railroad company. A vote on this matter was scheduled for March 1852, and the battle began. There was significant opposition to the railroad. Many in the county claimed that it was unnecessary, as goods produced locally could be taken beyond the county borders by carts. The arguments were fierce, and the vote was actually delayed until May to allow for more campaigning. In the end, the citizens of McDonough County voted to approve the stock purchase by a margin of 817 to 644.[9]

Even after the stock purchase was approved, though, there was no railroad. The Northern Cross' president, Judge Nehemiah Bushnell of Quincy, was unable to secure enough money from the eastern capitalists on whom he had relied, and in June 1853 it was decided that McDonough County would have to contribute an additional $25,000 to the railroad. This, and other fundraising efforts up and down the line, finally made construction of the railroad possible, which took place between 1853 and 1856. In October 1855 the first train ever to enter Macomb, the Northern Cross Railroad's locomotive *Fulton*, arrived from Quincy on the newly-built track. The line to Galesburg was completed in January 1856, and operations on the Northern Cross were merged with those on the Chicago & Aurora, after 1855 known as the Chicago

Burlington & Quincy, or CB&Q, and the Central Military Tract railroads.[10] Finally, Macomb had a permanent link to the outside world.

In the latter half of the 19th century, a railroad was often the deciding factor in whether a frontier town lived or died. The Northern Cross Railroad (which was foreclosed on in 1864 and sold to the CB&Q a year later) brought a tremendous amount of wealth and prosperity to the small village of Macomb. The population of McDonough County more than doubled in the ten years between 1850 and 1860, from 7,600 to 20,000, and a number of new towns grew up along the railroad tracks. Bardolph, Bushnell, Colchester, Tennessee, and Prairie City were all founded in the years that the railroad was being built. The promises that the railroad's promoters had made in the early 1850s all came true. Land prices in Macomb rose, the population increased, business for the town's merchants grew, and ease of shipment of materials dramatically modernized the way the townspeople did business.[11]

The construction of the railroad from Chicago to Quincy was part of a much larger trend. By the start of the Civil War there were over 3,500 miles of railroads in Illinois, and virtually every major population center was connected to a growing network of steel ribbons stretching across the state. After the end of the war the expansion continued. The Toledo Peoria & Western, McDonough County's second railroad, was constructed across the northern part of the county in the late 1860s. New railroads were being built all over, and by 1872 the railroad mileage in the state had increased to over 6,300 miles,[12] but for every new venture that was constructed it seemed that there were three that foundered before the first shovelful of earth was turned.

By the late 19th century the region south of Macomb which included Industry, Doddsville, and Littleton was one of the largest areas in western Illinois devoid of a railroad link. Within an

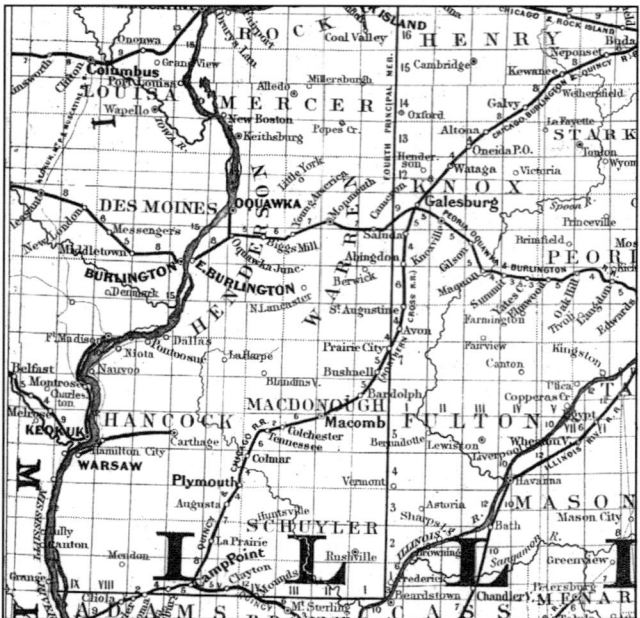

This 1861 railroad map of western Illinois shows the few railways through the Illinois Military Tract at the start of the Civil War. G. Woodworth Colton, "Railroad Map of Illinois."

area of about 500 square miles bordered by Macomb and Table Grove in the north, Plymouth and La Prairie in the west, Clayton and Mt. Sterling in the south, and Rushville and Vermont in the east, there was no way to get to the outside world except by horse. Perhaps because of this, numerous schemes for constructing a railroad through Industry and Littleton, the two largest towns in the gap, were brought before the people of this area in the 1880s and 1890s. They all failed.

Rail Road Excursion Trains!
FROM MACOMB TO QUINCY!
ON THE 24TH & 25TH INSTANT !!!
TO THE ADAMS COUNTY
AGRICULTURAL FAIR !

An advertisement from the 1850s picturing a Northern Cross train. WIU Special Collections.

One of the last of these plans, and likely the one that got the farthest before the turn of the century, was the line known as "Colonel Piper's Railroad." Colonel J.M. Piper was an entrepreneur from St. Louis who, in early 1895, proposed constructing a railroad that would extend from Macomb in the north, south to Grafton on the Mississippi, near the mouth of the Illinois River. From there it would connect with the already-existing Bluff Line and proceed directly into downtown St. Louis. The railroad would go through Industry, Camden, Mt. Sterling, Perry, Griggsville, Detroit, and Pearl, and at its southern end would traverse the length of Calhoun County, which, though bordered by the Mississippi and Illinois Rivers, lacked any rail link at all.[13]

Colonel Piper revealed his plans for the new railroad, which was officially called the St. Louis Perry & Chicago, at a meeting in Macomb on March 1, 1895. Three months later, the first major canvassing meeting was held to raise money for the venture. Forty thousand dollars in subscriptions would be required of the people of Macomb. A good number of civic-minded businessmen, including Albert Eads, Van L. Hampton, and J.M. Keefer of Macomb, and Amos S. Ellis and Joseph Lawyer of Industry, joined in the canvassing efforts that took place during the summer of 1895. But the man leading the drive for local support of the railroad was a man from Macomb named Charles Vilasco Chandler.[14]

Born in Macomb on January 25, 1843, C.V. Chandler was one of Colonel Charles and Sara C. Chandler's seven children. The Colonel was the owner and president of the First National Bank of Macomb, which brought in enough money for C.V. to get a good education. After his mother died in 1855, he attended boarding schools near Chicago and in Danbury, Connecticut. Instead of going off to college, in mid-1862 he returned to Illinois and enlisted in Company I of the 78th Illinois Volunteer Infantry to serve in the Civil War. He quickly ascended the ranks to Sergeant-Major and after nine months of service was already a Second Lieutenant.[15]

During September 1863 the 78th Illinois was part of Colonel John Mitchell's Brigade in the Army of the Cumberland, under General Thomas Rosecrans. They were marching in the vicinity of Rossville, Georgia, when, on September 19, the Battle of Chickamauga began. The bulk of both the Union and Confederate armies, including the 78th Illinois, were brought into the battle the next day. The Confederate armies under James Longstreet attacked in the morning, shattering the Union flank and driving back part of the army, but Union General George Thomas was able to rally his troops and stall the Confederate advance. With Thomas' outnumbered troops facing the high tide of the Rebel assault, two reserve brigades, one of which was Mitchell's brigade with the 78th Illinois, arrived at the moment of greatest need from the rear to support the Union line.[16]

This action of these two brigades saved the Army of the Cumberland from rout, helped to cement Thomas' reputation as the "Rock of Chickamauga," and resulted in forty percent of the men of the 78th Illinois being killed, wounded, or captured. Of the regiment's twenty officers, eight were casualties. C.V. Chandler was among them. At the height of the battle he was hit by a bullet which passed through one leg and into the other. After the battle he was promoted to Adjutant, but though he went through a period of recovery and briefly returned to duty, his wounds eventually forced him to resign on April 3, 1864.[17]

C.V. Chandler in a 1910-era portrait. Bateman & Shelby, The Historical Encyclopedia of Illinois and McDonough County.

After the war Chandler went to work for his father at the First National Bank. In 1866 he married Clara Baker, with whom he had six children. By 1870 he was elected city treasurer, beginning over four decades of public service in Macomb. Chandler's father died in 1878, making C.V. the bank's president. He continued to successfully operate the bank, reorganizing it in 1886 as the Bank of Macomb. Chandler was civically-minded, and he spearheaded several projects to improve the City of Macomb. By 1879, he had purchased all of the businesses in the block just south of the CB&Q freight house, demolished them, and created

Chandler Park for the enjoyment of the people of Macomb. Twenty years later, in 1899, he paid to build a monument to McDonough County's Civil War soldiers in Chandler Park.[18]

C.V. Chandler was one of the richest and most influential businessmen in Macomb, and his support for Colonel Piper's railroad was of tremendous importance. He initially subscribed for $1,000 worth of stock in the railroad (worth about $21,000 in inflation-adjusted 2005 money) and later added more to that amount. He served as Piper's primary contact person in McDonough County, the leader of the local efforts to support the railroad.[19]

The early signs seemed ominous to those in the Macomb area who were weary of empty promises made by railroad promoters. There was no construction work during the summer of 1895 until late August, when a handful of surveyors began laying out the locations of crossings for several east-west railroads. After this initial work was completed, there was again a lull in construction. Support for the project in McDonough County waned, and efforts by Piper to secure right-of-way from residents of Scotland Township in August and September met with resistance from wary farmers.[20]

Colonel Piper soldiered on and the St. Louis Perry & Chicago seemed to inch toward reality, but he was running out of time. In December the national economy entered a two-year recession that was something of an aftershock to the Panic of 1893. Prices fluctuated wildly, and the construction contractor informed Piper that another $500,000 was needed to build the railroad.[21]

Piper was desperate. In an apparent effort to raise more money, extensions to the railroad were promised including an east-west line through Bluffs and Barry and a northern extension all the way to Rock Island and Des Moines, Iowa. But it was all for naught. Though construction work began in a few random locations along the line in April 1896, by June it was evident that Piper's effort was foundering. In mid-June, Piper sold the railroad for $14,000 to the CB&Q, with

Macomb's Civil War monument, which was sponsored and paid for by C.V. Chandler. WIU Special Collections.

Industry Enterprise: "Piper's Railroad. Our poetical editor, who has been in the cupola for the last eight months looking for the coming of Piper's new railroad, crawled down from his perch this week and penned the following:

Come and stand around us,
Although it hurts your head,
And we will try and tell you
Some things that Piper said.

They stood and looked upon him
With wistful, eager eyes,
And said to one another
I'm afraid he's telling lies.

Yes, Piper came to Industry
And said it was all so
That we would have a railroad,
But we guess it is no go.

Now Piper, he was with us
On the Fourth day of July
And said he'd come next year
On the early morn "Eli."

He said unto our farmers-
"Its the very thing you need:
Then you can ship your grain
And everything you feed."

He said unto our merchants,
Which sounded good and great:
"You can sell much cheaper then
On account of reduced freight."

He said unto our druggists
Words we didn't get to hear,
But we're of the opinion
That he asked if they kept beer.

He said unto our painters,
Although 'twas very faint:
"You must remember, boys,
The depot and round-house is to paint."

He said to "Father Rayburn,"
And it sounded like a charm,
"That he'd be worth a million
If he'd only plat his farm."

He said unto our landlord,
And we feared 'twould cause a muss:
"Now Joel, save the dollars,
For you will need a 'bus."

He said unto the doctor,
And it sounded rather funny-
"Doc, I wish you'd keep them well
Until I get their money."

He said unto the dead beats
That loaf the whole year round,
"Remember, there'll be work to do
When the railroad comes to town."

He said unto our carpenters-
Creel, Laughlin and Bill West-
"There will be many bridges to build
And you want to do your best."

He said to our cigarmaker
To live in faith and hope,
For when the engines came to town
That everyone will smoke.

He said unto John Lickey,
Although we think it thin,
"The cars will kill a dozen a year
And that will make 'biz' for him."

He said to the committee,
Which numbered five or six,
"Remember, boys, to tell them
'Twill be here in ninety-six."

He said unto the printer,
But here our face we hide,
"If we would help to boom the road
'Twould cost nothing for us to ride."

He said to unbelievers
Whom he termed as arrant fools,
That the contract was already let
To those six hundred mules.

He said to a confidential,
But here we hate to tell,
"If I get the twenty thousand
I'll bust them sure as h--l." [sic]

And now my story is ended,
We hope in peace to abide,
But if Piper builds the railroad
We will all take a ride."

From the November 8, 1895, Macomb Daily Journal.

which it would have competed directly for traffic headed north out of St. Louis. Predictably, by the end of 1896, the Burlington had quashed the entire project. Residents of Macomb, Industry, and the other towns to the south would have to wait for their railroad.[22]

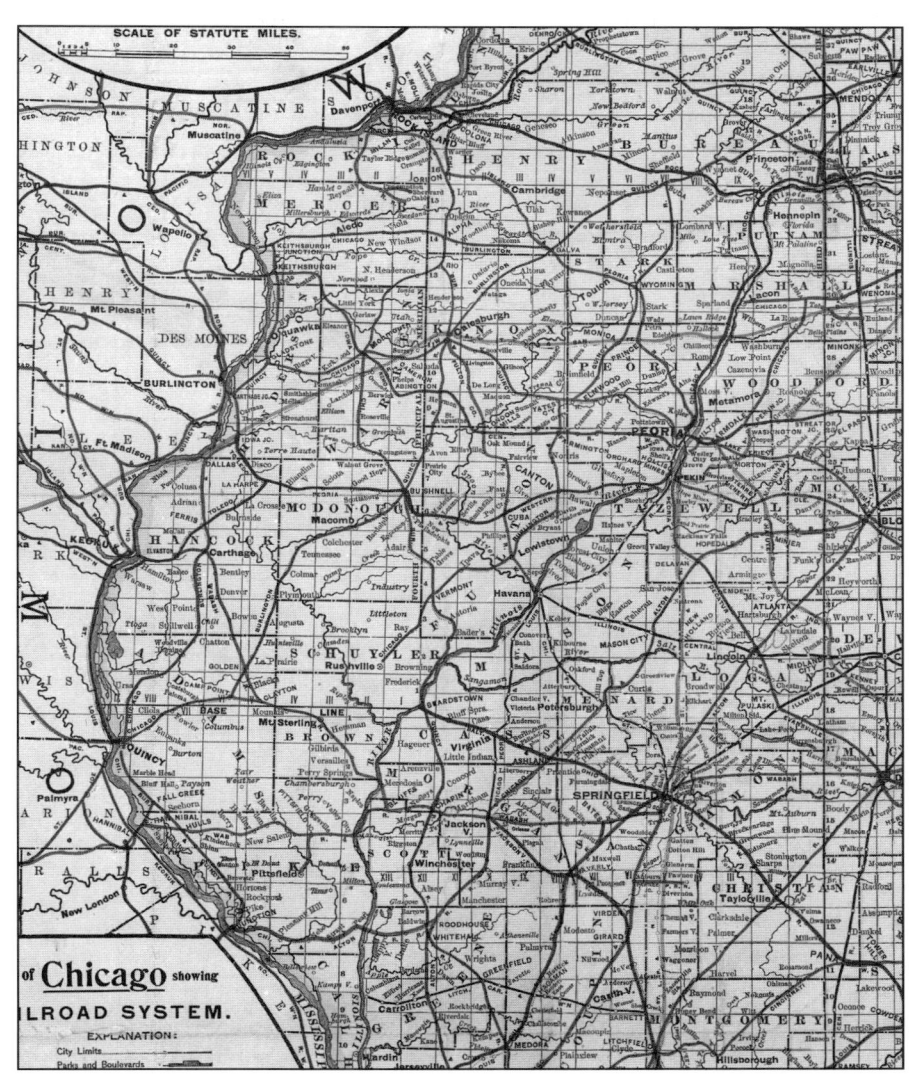

By 1898, western Illinois was served by a vast network of railway lines almost inconceivable fifty years earlier. Rock Island is at top center, Macomb just left of center. Rand, McNally & Company, "Railroad Map of Illinois."

The Electric Road

The final push to build a railroad south from Macomb originated in late 1901 with William Alexander Compton, a Macomb resident. Compton was born on March 5, 1864, south of Macomb in Scotland Township. Educated at the Macomb Normal College, he graduated in 1885, and after studying law, was admitted to the bar in 1888. He later founded a successful and profitable real estate business and was elected to the Illinois state legislature as the 28th District Representative in 1896.[1] In November 1901 Compton enlisted the support of H.G. Tunstall, a man from New York City who represented a group of venture capitalists interested in seeing a railroad built from Macomb to Industry, Rushville, and Beardstown. What made this proposal different from all that had come before it was electricity. The New Yorkers were unwilling to consider a steam railroad, but rather insisted that the new line be an electric interurban road.[2] Electric traction was just entering maturity at the turn of the century, and most major cities had rapidly expanding networks of streetcar lines within their borders. The interurban, or inter-city electric railway, was a newer phenomenon developed in the last years of the 19th century. More powerful electric motors and controls made it possible to run high-speed electric trains over long distances, creating the possibility for a nationwide network of

The M&WI's gas-electric box-cab motor is seen here in 1904 at the north end of the railroad, at the corner of Jackson and Johnson streets in Macomb. The Catholic school is in the background. Lumber is being loaded onto a boxcar right in the street. WIU Special Collections.

William Alexander Compton in a 1913-era portrait. Bateman & Shelby, The Historical Encyclopedia of Illinois and McDonough County.

interurbans to rival the steam railroads.

The people of McDonough and Schuyler counties were enthusiastic about the idea of such a modern railroad being constructed locally. Pro-railroad efforts centered around Industry, where civic boosters like Philander Avery and Amos S. Ellis joined the effort to canvass the area for money, and gather support for the project. On November 13, 1901, the Macomb & Western Illinois Railway (M&WI) was incorporated and directors William Compton (President), J.M. Keefer (Vice President), Ralph S. Chandler (Secretary and Treasurer), Isaac M. Fellheimer, Albert Eads, and Willis I. Hitt were appointed to the Board of Directors. The next day a large meeting was held at Industry to announce the plan for the railroad. Though the line would eventually run to Beardstown, the segment from Macomb to Industry would be built first and put into operation before construction would continue south. Most of the M&WI directors were present at the meeting. C.V. Chandler, however, was in Quincy chairing the annual reunion of the 78th Illinois, but he sent a letter expressing his support for the project. It was decided that the residents of the Industry area would have to raise $30,000 toward the cost of the railroad. At a similar meeting in Scotland Township two weeks later, it was announced that the residents living in the areas south of Macomb would have to raise an additional $12,000.[3]

It wasn't easy to raise that much money in an area with a total population of fewer than 1,000 people (adjusted for inflation, $42,000 in 1902 was the equivalent of about $930,000 in 2005 money). By late January 1902 it was apparent that the canvassing committees in Industry and Scotland Township weren't going to be able to raise that large an amount of money, so the requirement was changed. If $50,000 could be raised along the entire route, including from Macomb itself, the railroad would still be built. In a meeting at Industry on January 28, it was agreed to increase Macomb's share to $25,000, reducing the amount of money Industry and Scotland Township would have to raise by one-third.[4]

By May 1902, the $25,000 expected of the southern part of the county had been raised, and Chandler, Compton, and others were hard at work canvassing within Macomb. On June 27, S.B. Downer, a civil engineer from Michigan who had previous experience laying out electric lines in Michigan and Illinois, arrived in Macomb and began work on surveying the route from Macomb to Industry. Two different routes were surveyed. The east route left downtown Macomb headed straight east along Jackson Street and turned south to follow the approximate current alignment of Route 67. The west route left the city near the county fairgrounds at Johnson and Grant streets and went south from there, turning east toward Industry about eight miles south of Macomb. A streetcar line to the Western Illinois State Normal School on the northwest side of town was also planned. Surveying and cost estimates were completed by mid-July without much trouble, though the location of the depot in Industry couldn't be agreed on. By September construction still had not begun, and it wasn't until the first week of October that the company formally announced that it had settled on the western route, and had secured most of the right-of-way it needed.[5]

At 8:20 a.m. on October 16, 1902, the wife of M&WI Vice President W.H. Rayburn turned the first shovelful of dirt on the new electric railway in a ceremony held on a part of the right-of-way located on James Scudder's farm two miles west of Industry. Of the one hundred people in attendance, William Compton was one of only a handful not from Industry. As soon as the ceremony was done, grading work was begun by ten teams with plows and wheeled scrapers.[6]

The next two months saw slow progress in grading while the railroad's officers were involved in land condemnation proceedings in the courts. As a railroad, the M&WI had the right of eminent domain, and could seize any land it needed for its right-of-way. Unfortunately, in cases where a fair price for the land could not be agreed upon, the courts had to set the price themselves. While the vast majority of the farmers along the railroad were happy to donate or sell the land the railroad would need at a nominal price, there were a few who insisted on a higher price.

President Compton purchased more wheeled scrapers in late November, and by mid-December there were two grading gangs at work. Web Kirkbride's gang, with twelve scrapers, was working north of Camp Creek while a second gang of fifteen scrapers under Philander Avery was working on the northwest side of Industry. It was tough work in spots as the grade heading out of Industry was eighteen feet high and over thirty feet wide at the base.[7]

At the same time, citizens south of Industry were taking notice of the work being done to the north. After consulting with Compton, they got a promise from the M&WI that if they could raise $20,000, the initial segment of the railroad would be extended from Industry to Littleton. At a meeting in November chaired by James Little, a canvassing committee in Littleton was appointed to raise the money.[8]

In January 1903, work came to a standstill as the frozen ground could not be effectively moved. Despite the cold, pile-driving began on the bridges over Grindstone and Camp Creeks in February. In late March the railroad's first injury occurred when Lowrey Avery received a scalp wound, when a piling he was working on sprung back and hit him in the head.[9]

Grading began again in March at several points along the line. By May there were 30 scrapers in operation, and work began at the northern end of the line, with the workers quartered at the fairgrounds in Macomb. Progress was still slow, and concerns began to rise about the timetable for completion. The railroad's estimates for the time it would take the construction force to complete a section of the grade were repeatedly shown to be overly optimistic, and it appeared possible that the railroad might not be in operation by January 1, 1904, as promised. The danger in this was that the $50,000 that had been raised from the local citizens was contingent on the railroad being in operation between Macomb and Industry by this date. If it was not running by then, the people who had subscribed money would no longer be contractually bound to pay up. It was also pointed out that construction had not begun on the power house, which would be needed to provide electricity for the line's interurban cars.[10]

Chandler and Compton continued undaunted, though. In June they met with the canvassing committee in Littleton, which had been unable to raise the $20,000 asked of it, and discussed proposals for extending the M&WI regardless. Surveyors were already laying out a route between Industry and Littleton, and the railroad agreed to extend south to Littleton as long as the scheduled completion date was extended from January 1904, to September 1904. Just days later, on June 27, the Macomb Mt. Sterling & Beardstown Railway was incorporated for the purpose of extending the M&WI from Littleton to Mt. Sterling and Beardstown.[11]

Grading work continued through the summer with a force of about forty scrapers. Most of the work concentrated on a few areas that required large fills, particularly the approaches to Camp Creek, and on the northwest side of Industry. Unfortunately the bridge work was going very slowly, so the M&WI hired a man from New York to run the pile-driver, and brought on Jack O. Moon of Colchester to head up the gang of car-

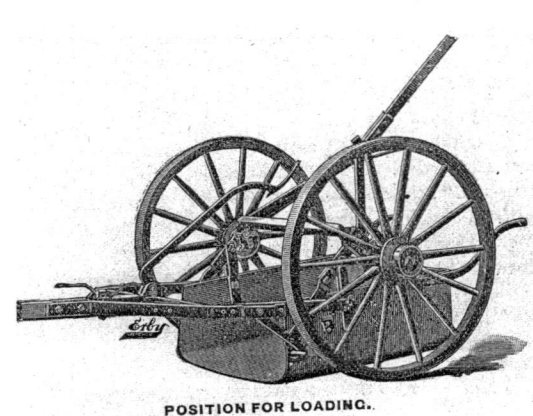

POSITION FOR LOADING.

Most of the railroad right-of-way was graded using horse-drawn Western Wheeled Scrapers like this one. Courtesy of the Aurora Historical Society.

penters building the bridges. In August, with concerns about the slow progress mounting, Compton purchased more wheeled scrapers, bringing the number of wheeled scrapers in use by the M&WI to sixty-three. By the end of August, at the height of the grading work, the company had 160 horses and 125 men working on the grading and bridge work at several sites up and down the line from Macomb to Industry.[12]

At the beginning of September, the grading gangs began to be moved south of Industry to begin work on the Industry-Littleton segment of the railroad. The last gang at work north of Industry was a large group working on grading the approaches to Camp Creek, work that had begun back in late 1902, and still hadn't been completed. In mid-September one of the workers, a Bohemian immigrant, disappeared during a period of heavy flooding and was presumed drowned in Camp Creek. The work continued, and the job was finally finished and the work force moved south of Industry near the end of the month.[13]

The grading work south of Industry was not any easier, but the company now had all sixty-three scrapers and a force of experienced men concentrated together. It took a month to hack through a large stand of timber south of Industry and more time to create a twenty-seven foot deep cut, the deepest on the entire route. An additional two weeks was needed for the workforce under Dave Justus to grade a cut through the timber stand that was nicknamed "Blue Cut," because it took so long to grade that it gave the workers the blues. By the end of October, major grading work south of Industry was completed after only two months. Most of the grading crews were laid off, and the remaining workers moved back to the northern end of the route to finish leveling the grade, and to do the grading needed within the Macomb city limits.[14]

It was at this point, in mid-November, that arrangements for the railroad's financing were finalized. A $300,000 mortgage was filed for the railroad's property with the county circuit clerk, with a bond issue by the railroad to the American Trust and Savings Bank of Chicago. The 300 bonds were each $1,000 40-year bonds with 5% annual interest. The amount of money it had cost to build the railroad, $300,000, was the equivalent of approximately $6.4 million in inflation-adjusted 2005 money. The problem with the bond issue was that buyers for most of the bonds could not be found, so the majority of them ended up in the hands of the Bank of Macomb, owned by C.V. Chandler.[15]

Once major grading was done, work moved quickly. A ditch wide enough for the crossties and deep enough that the track could be laid with the railhead at street level was cut down the length of Johnson Street from Jackson Street to a point just south of St. Francis Hospital, where the railroad entered private right-of-way on the west side of the road. It was planned to lay tracks from the corner of Jackson and Johnson Streets east down Jackson Street to the square, from there north on Lafayette Street to Calhoun Street, and thence east on Calhoun Street to the old CB&Q depot near Randolph Street. No grading was ever done on this route, though, and the rails never got east of Johnson

> This road will surely go, and if it only goes to Littleton and we do not get it here, it will cripple Rushville quite badly. Macomb merchants are making good in the north part of the county. Already are Macomb papers being circulated in that part of the county, from Ray to Camden, and in these papers are big advertisements of Macomb merchants. People of the north part of the county are turning to Macomb, for they will have easier access to that city and the railroad is rapidly pulling everything toward Macomb. To be sure Macomb is a good town and has hustling, up-to-date merchants and business men who are looking for a graft like this, which is all good and proper, but don't we want this trade worse than they? But how are you going to keep it? By seeing that this railroad is graded to Rushville before a tie or rail is laid along the route. Great stacks of ties are strewn along the line now, and as fast as surfacing is done these will be put down. No it is up to Rushville, and if the business men want to hold their own let them be up and doing. Hold a mass meeting and devise a means of securing this railroad. In looking at this work going on one can see the great strides Macomb is making for Schuyler patronage, and their efforts are bound to win if Rushville don't wake up and take a hand.
>
> *From the Schuyler Citizen, as reprinted in the 3 October 1903, Macomb Daily Journal.*

Street. On November 2, 1903, the first of what would eventually be over 100 carloads of construction supplies arrived. Cars of cedar ties from Michigan and 30-foot rails of 60 lb. weight (per yard) started to arrive on the Burlington along with cars of spikes, bolts, angle bars, and switch components. On November 17, the Reverend James H. Morgan of the Presbyterian Church drove the first spike in Macomb, and the construction contractor's crew got to work. On November 22, the railroad's first piece of rolling stock, a small 0-4-4T Forney steam locomotive originally built for the Chicago elevated, arrived on the Burlington and was swiftly put into service hauling supplies from the temporary interchange with the CB&Q that had been built on North Johnson Street, to the steel gangs laying rail at the south end of town. By November 25, track had been laid past the city limits, and a week later the steel gangs were nearing Camp Creek.[16]

Opinions differed on whether the railroad would be completed to Industry on schedule, December 1903, and would be able to collect the money that had been raised. The *Macomb Daily Journal*, a supporter of the railroad, predicted that the railroad would not be completed to Industry until early January, but that most people who had signed promissory notes would overlook the technical discrepancy and pay the money anyway. "The Journal makes this counter forecast to croakers' predictions, because it does not believe that the note-signers are a set of Shylocks, who claim the 'exact execution of the bond,' or else 'a pound of flesh nearest the heart.'" The *Industry Enterprise* took a more optimistic tack, predicting that the railroad might, with a burst of effort, be able to complete track all the way to Littleton by the end of the year.[17]

By the fourth week in December it became obvious that the railroad would be in Industry on time. The railroad's first passenger car arrived from the St. Louis Car Company on December 17. It had to be pulled by a locomotive, but was constructed so that electrical equipment could be easily fitted to it later to make it self-propelled. On December 23, the rails reached their goal at last: the residents of Industry finally had a railroad. Later that day the Industry depot, which had been framed in Macomb, was loaded on one of the construction trains and taken to Industry to be set up and finished. The railroad got a Christmas present early, when on December 24, a small gasoline-powered locomotive was switched onto M&WI rails from the CB&Q. This diminutive engine, which was one of the very first internal-combustion railway locomotives ever put into use, was called the "electric motor" or simply "the motor" by the M&WI, and was intended to be its ticket to fulfilling the requirement in its franchise that it not operate steam locomotives on a permanent basis.[18] The railroad didn't have enough money to string electric wire along its route, but hauling trains with this gas-electric motor would make it possible to do away with steam. Because of this, the railroad would still be popularly known as the "electric road."

Clarence Vial (in cab), James Ira Hodges and Roy Sullivan pose with the M&WI gas-electric motor at the corner of Jackson & Johnson in Macomb in 1904. WIU Special Collections.

The days after Christmas saw a virtual halt to construction operations. As of December 23, the construction crews had been "striking a 'bee-line' for Littleton like the very Old Scratch was at the heels of every tie-man and rail-man on the job," as the *Macomb Daily Journal* put it, but when the steam engine went dead on Christmas Day, construction at the south end of the line was temporarily halted. On December 29, the directors and officers of the M&WI were taken on an inspection trip to Industry by the motor hauling the passenger car. The next day, December 30, 1903, the Macomb & Western Illinois opened for business. The first train left for Industry at 8:30 in the morning. The years of work, and the hundreds of thousands of dollars that had gone into constructing a railroad south from Macomb, had not been in vain. The railroad had finally arrived.[19]

Operations in the first few months were spotty. The motor, though brand new, was terribly unreliable and was continually breaking down. The only other locomotive was the 0-4-4T Forney, which often had to abandon the task of pulling construction trains to the south end of the line and instead perform yeoman duty on passenger runs to Industry. Track construction continued south from Industry and reached Littleton on January 31, 1903. By the end of February passenger service was extended to the south end of the line and stockyards were erected in Littleton. On February 26, the M&WI acquired its second passenger car, a coach designed as a streetcar but without electrical motors and equipment. With the arrival of the second car, a standard schedule was established in which car number 1 was used north of Industry, and car number 2 was used between Industry and Littleton. The electric motor was being used, between mechanical failures at least, for all passenger service.[20]

The railroad almost immediately began to encounter serious operating problems. Derailments were frequent owing to the poor and lightweight rails and crossties and lack of track ballast, and with the spring thaw the railroad experienced numerous washouts of the roadbed. In late March, there was a suspension of service due to poor roadbed conditions. So much of the embankment at Camp Creek had washed away that the ties were projecting out past the grade thirty feet above the water. On March 29, the steam engine derailed just south of Camp Creek, damaging its air brake and putting it out of service. The next week, service was suspended indefinitely until the track gangs could repair the right-of-way sufficiently to allow safe passage of trains.[21]

After three months of service, the M&WI was already experiencing serious setbacks. The electric motor it had purchased had proven to be an almost complete failure, although the general consensus was that internal-combustion engines of its type would "eventually do away with the trolley

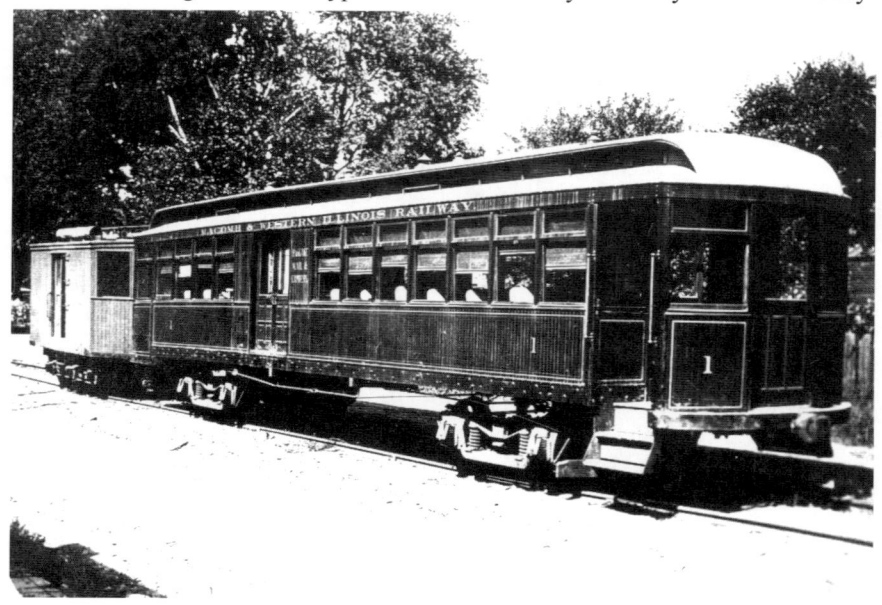

The railroad's first passenger car, combine 1, seen here in 1904 being pulled north on Johnson Street by the gas-electric motor. WIU Special Collections.

> A story has just come to light on W.A. Compton, the president of the Macomb and Western Illinois railroad, which proves that the company is accommodating and obliging to the public. In addition to stopping along the way and allowing people to get on or off the train as they desire, a new courtesy has just been related. The incident happened one day while Mr. Compton was acting as conductor. He was just ready to pull out with his train for Industry, and had, in a dignified manner that would make old railroad conductors blush, exclaimed, "all aboard," when his attention was called to a young lady running toward the train and making wild jestures [sic] with her hands, as if she wanted to board the train. By this time the motor had begun to move and Mr. Compton signaled it to stop. The young lady kept up her pace, running toward the train like a fire department and Mr. Compton had stepped down on the platform to assist her into the car, when to his surprise she rushed by him and made for a car window, that had just been raised and planted a kiss on the cheek of a young man, who had been a silent spectator, and bade him goodbye, asking him to "come up again next Sunday." This started the laugh on the conductor and had all the occupants of the car been men he might have "cussed," but instead he remarked that was the first time he ever saw an entire railroad system held up until a girl could run two blocks to kiss her fellow goodbye. As we have no desire to incur the ill will of the young man, and at the same time cause trouble between him and his Industry girl, we refrain from giving his name.
> *From the January 22, 1904, Macomb Daily Journal.*

wire or third rail." The problem was simply that it was too underpowered to be of much use even on the moderate grades of the M&WI. The motor could not manage to pull more than a single coach or freight car and, even with one coach, could not make good enough time to keep to the passenger schedule. As late as early April 1904, the motor was still being shown off, when a group of CB&Q officials took it on a test run to Bardolph, but in May the M&WI constructed a permanent water tower in Industry and confirmed that it planned to use its diminutive steam engine for all future passenger trains. The motor would be retained for use primarily within the Macomb city limits, since the railroad's municipal ordinance did not allow the use of steam engines in town. Every passenger train would undergo a "power change" at St. Francis Hospital south of town where the steam engine would be exchanged for the motor, and the motor would take the trains from the edge of town up to Jackson Street.[22]

Operations continued between Macomb and Littleton, beginning at the end of April, when service was restored over the repaired right-of-way. On May 1, the connection between the M&WI and the Burlington was removed from North Johnson Street, as it had been a temporary connection only and the company was not allowed to keep its tracks laid on North Johnson. The railroad was cut back on Johnson Street to Jackson Street, where on the southeast corner of the intersection a modest waiting room had been created in the front room of a blacksmith shop. This severed the railroad's connection with the national rail network and made it impossible to interchange freight cars. In other words, any freight carried along the M&WI had to be unloaded at Macomb and loaded back into CB&Q freight cars a few hundred feet away.[23]

The railroad considered this situation intolerable, but the property owners along the block and a half of North Johnson Street would not permit the railroad to be rebuilt along that stretch of the street. The result was that in late July, the M&WI developed plans to build a belt line around the west side of Macomb. The new branch, whose sole purpose was to make it possible to interchange freight cars with the CB&Q, left the M&WI main line just south of St. Francis Hospital south of Macomb. It angled off in a northwesterly direction to the West Sewerpipe Works, which was located about two blocks west of Ward Street on the south side of the CB&Q, and already had an interchange with the Burlington.[24]

The problem was that the M&WI was virtually incapable of continuing normal operations until the west side belt line was completed. In early August the steam engine failed, leaving the M&WI with only the unreliable motor to haul trains, and with a tough decision. The decision it made became the first shot fired in what would later be called by the *Macomb Daily Journal* the "railroad war." On August 9, when several of the railroad's most vociferous critics living along North Johnson Street were out of town at a Republican convention in Bushnell, the railroad laid a temporary track along North Johnson Street to connect its rails to the Burlington. The impetus was the need to send the Forney steam engine out for repairs and to bring onto the M&WI a leased Burlington steam engine to replace it, but the connection was not removed after this exchange was complete. Freight cars and trains of construction materials for the west side belt line, on which construction was just beginning, regularly traversed the new trackage on North Johnson Street in clear defiance of the railroad's original ordinance.[25]

The property owners who had opposed the railroad's presence on the streets of Macomb were not happy. They tried to swear out arrest warrants against the railroad's managers, but soon realized that it was technically a mu-

M&WI locomotive 1 poses with a work train at Littleton around 1904. Jesse Hodges (third from left) is crew foreman, with James Ira Hodges (second from right) engineer and Charlie Elting (far right) fireman. WIU Special Collections.

M&WI engine 1 poses with coach 2 and crew at Macomb Yards around 1904 (the grandstands at the county fairgrounds are in the right background). L-R: Conductor James Ira Hodges, Fireman Ed Smithers, Engineer Tom Hendrickson and son, and Roy "Happy Hooligan" Ransom. WIU Special Collections.

nicipal issue. Therefore, on October 11, Superintendent of Streets S.P. Danley served notice on the officers of the M&WI to remove their tracks from North Johnson Street immediately. Two days later they received President Compton's response. The M&WI was not going to remove its tracks, and any effort on the part of the city to remove them would be viewed as unlawful. The reason was that the M&WI was engaged in hauling mail from Macomb to Littleton, which meant that removal of any railroad trackage was impeding the carriage of mail and was a violation of federal law. That same day Compton sent workers out to double-spike the tracks on North Johnson Street, making it virtually impossible for city workers to tear up the tracks without heavy specialized equipment. For the moment, the railroad had won. Its connection with the Burlington on North Johnson Street was secure.[26]

Improvements were being made on the M&WI at a rapid pace during the summer and fall of 1904. The water tower at Industry was completed in late May and was soon followed by a small house for a handcar. In September stockyards were built just north of the depot there. In October a permanent depot was finally built in Littleton, following the grain elevator which had just recently been constructed there. Condemnation proceedings to seize land for the west side belt line in Macomb continued in court until early October, by which time construction was already well underway. Most of the belt line traversed level ground, but a 400-foot-long trestle had to be built through low-

> Since the new railroad has been put in operation a debt of gratitude has been paid by the president of the road which will make both friends and enemies think more of Mr. Compton than though he had done nothing to prove his gratitude to the young man who saved the Compton household from the loss of their only child in a watery grave in Kiljordan. Most of our readers are aware of the accident which befell the little fellow, some four years ago next February, when he fell into the water and would have been drowned had it not been for the prompt and heroic act of Jas. Hodges. The creek was bank full and much ice was floating down. The child was standing on a bridge, and becoming dizzy fell in. The mother, who was close by, tried in vain to rescue her child and she ran down the bank screaming for help. At the critical moment Hodges, who has made his way in the world as a hired hand, having worked for some time near Industry, came driving at a rapid rate, being attracted by the heartrending screams of the mother. He did not hesitate, but left his team standing and ran to the water's edge and plunged in about ten feet in front of the child and thus took him from what would have been a watery grave. He worked for some little time with the boy to bring him to consciousness and then carried him to the Compton home, leaving for his home before Mr. Compton arrived from his office. When Mr. Compton met Mr. Hodges he thanked him for his kindness and on parting assured him that he would remember him in the future. Nothing more was said of the matter between the two men until the company was ready to start the passenger train on the new road when Mr. Compton sent for his benefactor and informed him that he now had a chance to partly remunerate him for the act he did in saving the life of his child and gave him a job as porter and brakeman on the new coach. Mr. Hodges was surprised and glad to know that he had been remembered. It was indeed a glad time for both. Mr. Compton seemed to be as glad of the chance to repay his debt of gratitude as Mr. Hodges was glad to know that he was to have a good job. Everybody who has learned the above facts applauded Mr. Compton for giving the job to the right man. Thus two men are made happy, each because he did his duty to his fellow man, one with no thought of reward or any other thing except saving the life that was in peril and the other to show his appreciation. The Enterprise hopes to see Mr. Hodges make an efficient employee and remain with the road for years.
> *From the Industry Enterprise, reprinted in the January 15, 1904, Macomb Daily Journal.*

Conductor James Ira Hodges (left) is surrounded by well-dressed young ladies in this interior view of M&WI coach 2 taken around 1904. WIU Special Collections.

lying ground just north of Grant Street, in what is now Patton Park. The railroad was also building a small yard and a 128 foot long engine house at the junction of the two lines just south of St. Francis Hospital, a location which would come to be known as the Macomb Yards.[27]

On October 19, C.V. Chandler told the *Macomb Daily Journal* that the railroad "would be willing to give any reasonable guarantee to the city or individuals that we will remove the track [on North Johnson Street] by Jan. 1 [1905]," saying the connection to the CB&Q was "indispensable." The city council held him to it. By early December, Chandler had been persuaded to give the city a $10,000 bond guaranteeing the tracks would be gone from North Johnson Street by January 1. Chandler kept his word. The 400-foot trestle was completed by the first week of December, and by the end of the month work had been completed on the belt line. The M&WI removed the tracks from North Johnson Street on December 30, 1904. From then on, the tracks along Johnson Street from the Macomb Yards north to Jackson Street would be used solely by passenger trains hauled by the motor, and freight trains would use the west side belt line to interchange with the CB&Q.[28]

The next day, New Year's Eve 1904, was one of the worst days in the railroad's short but tortured history. Around 6 p.m. that evening, the engine house at the Macomb Yards caught fire and burned to the ground. The engine house contained the motor, and it was completely destroyed. Furthermore, the leased Burlington steam engine was severely damaged, and it had to be towed to Galesburg to be rebuilt. The cause of the fire was never definitively determined. There was no insurance and the cost of the damage was estimated to be about $4,000. The motor was not replaced, though a secondhand 4-4-0 steam engine had coincidentally been purchased earlier that same day in Chicago to supplement the railroad's small Forney.[29]

Two days after the fire, the "railroad war" continued at the Macomb city council meeting when several aldermen tried unsuccessfully to repeal entirely the ordinance granting the M&WI the right to run trains within the city limits. The effort failed, but two weeks later St. Paul's Catholic Church, which owned the property on the southwest corner of Jackson and Johnson Streets, brought suit against the M&WI for $100,000 in damages. The church argued that the railroad interfered with access to the church and was an "annoyance" and "great inconvenience." The barrage of opposition to the railroad continued when in late April, before the Catholic church's suit against the railroad could even be tried in court, another suit was brought against the M&WI. Property owners living along South Johnson Street, led by James W. Stuart, filed a lawsuit which asked for $7,500 in monetary damages. It was also a mandamus suit that aimed to compel the removal of the M&WI entirely from within the city limits of Macomb.[30]

Operations continued on the M&WI while the pending lawsuits waited for their day in court. Business was fair and growing. In 1905, a coal mine was built on the south side of Littleton adjacent to the M&WI which, at its peak, produced about 1,500 bushels of coal each day. Most of the coal was sold locally, the rest was taken north on the railroad. Passenger service was booming and the railroad was making a profit of as much as $2,000-$3,000 per month. The $30,000 cost of constructing the west side belt line had added to the road's debt, but the condition of the roadbed had been largely stabilized and trains were running on time. Management was still publicly advertising plans to extend southward toward Mt. Sterling or Beardstown. It seemed that the railroad's biggest problems on the horizon were the two cases pending in court, of which the first, the mandamus suit brought by James W. Stuart, was considered in June 1906. Judge Grier refused to dismiss the case, saying that if the plaintiffs could prove their claims that the petition to allow the construction of the M&WI along Johnson Street didn't have enough signatures for the city council to legally issue the ordinance, then the tracks would have to be torn up. In September 1906, the court denied an application by St. Paul's Catholic Church for an injunction that would prevent the M&WI from operating steam engines within the city limits, which it had been doing on its passenger trains since the destruction of the motor in the December 1904 engine house fire.[31]

Despite its legal victory, the beleaguered M&WI had not seen the last of its troubles. Although it had been making an operating profit, it was still $300,000 in debt due to its construction costs. This debt was supported by C.V. Chandler through his Bank of Macomb, which held nearly all of the railroad's stock. Chandler was one of the richest men in town, and he was the financial backer to a number of local ventures. Of these the M&WI was paramount. However, by constructing the railroad to Littleton, he had overextended himself. On the last day of November 1906, completely without warning, the Bank of Macomb did not open its doors. Chandler didn't have enough cash with which to do business, and he closed the bank until assets could be sold to raise the money needed. Suddenly the future of Macomb's "Electric Road" seemed in doubt.[32]

M&WI engine 1 is hauling the road's entire passenger roster of two cars in this shot taken at Industry around 1904. WIU Special Collections.

In The Balance

Over the course of the next week, the finances of the Bank of Macomb were made public. C.V. Chandler made it apparent that the bank's cash shortfall was due almost entirely to the fact that it had been forced to single-handedly finance most of the construction of the M&WI, and that it had been unable to resell the railroad's bonds due to the barrage of litigation against the road. Of the bank's financial resources, which totaled $566,000, $239,000 were tied up in the M&WI. The bank's liabilities amounted to some $455,000. The fact that the bank would be entirely unable to pay its debts unless it could realize at least $100,000 from the sale of M&WI bonds or property must not have been lost on Chandler, but he made reassuring promises to the depositors of his bank and there was little sense of panic that the bank would actually become insolvent. The Bank of Macomb was actually owned by C.V. Chandler & Company, a banking firm comprised of C.V. Chandler and his wife Clara, which also owned the Bank of Bardolph and was co-owner of the Bank of Colchester. On December 19, 1906, Chandler sold the Bank of Bardolph to a group of locals, ridding himself of that burden, but already there were concerns that the M&WI might be in danger. In December, President Compton of the M&WI made a statement that unless $50,000 worth of the railroad's bonds were bought by the citizens of Macomb, Industry, and Little-

The above photo, taken at Industry around 1910, shows engine 4 hauling a single combine northbound. WIU Special Collections.

The three photos on this and the facing page were taken of the wreck at Industry in 1907. Above, engine 2 lies on its side with the boxcar jackknifed across the track in front of it. Below, the tender is shown derailed and partly overturned behind the locomotive. Note the curious townspeople of Industry surrounding the wreck in these pictures, and the steam apparently still escaping from the wrecked locomotive. Both photographs were taken on January 25, from the east side of the tracks. Opposite, the CB&Q wrecker (background) hauls the locomotive back onto the tracks on January 26. This photo looks northeast. WIU Special Collections.

ton, the current management might not be able to retain control of the railroad. This call was ignored.[1]

The year 1907 was not a good one for the M&WI. The bad luck began on January 25, when the only serious wreck in the railroad's history occurred at Industry. Engineer Edward Harvey and fireman James Ira Hodges were running locomotive number 2 northbound, and they were about a quarter mile south of the Industry depot when the boxcar they were pushing derailed and was thrown sideways across the tracks. The locomotive collided with it and overturned, injuring Hodges and badly damaging the engine. There were no other serious injuries, but it took two days for a crane rented from the CB&Q to clear the wreck, and the loss of one of the railroad's only two steam engines was no small problem.[2]

Less than a month later one of the pending court cases, the suit brought by St. Paul's Catholic Church to prevent the M&WI from using steam engines on the streets of Macomb, came before the Illinois State Supreme Court in Springfield. In this matter the railroad was successful. The court found that the railroad was subject to the will of the property owners along its route, but not to the church alone.[3]

But the second lawsuit, the mandamus action brought by James W. Stuart that aimed to force the removal of the railroad from the streets of Macomb entirely, came before the county circuit court at the end of May, and this time the railroad lost. Judge Gray found that the railroad had not conformed to its franchise, not by operating steam engines within Macomb, an action specifically prohibited by the municipal franchise, but rather by ending the tracks at Jackson and Johnson Streets and not extending them all the way to

Lafayette Street as had been originally stipulated. The railroad was given one year to remove its tracks from within the city of Macomb. The effect on the railroad was potentially disastrous. Without its line into the city, it would be impossible to pick up or drop off passengers closer than one mile from the center of the city, a severe inconvenience that would be sure to harm the railroad's passenger business markedly. But worse was to come. On June 8, 1907, a week after the court ruling came down, involuntary bankruptcy proceedings against C.V. Chandler & Company were initiated in federal court in Peoria.[4]

The bankruptcy proceedings had been initiated by a group of three of the Bank of Macomb's creditors who claimed that Chandler had shown preference to other creditors in the partial payments he had made on his debts thus far. Over the next two weeks attorneys on both sides met and were able to hammer out a deal which would avoid bankruptcy court. The Bank of Macomb and the Chandlers individually would put all of their property, business and personal, under the control of a committee of the bank's creditors which would then determine the quickest and best way to convert the assets into cash. Included in the arrangement were the bank's M&WI stocks and bonds, consisting of all of the railroad's stock and most of its bonds. This arrangement initially seemed to work out, but in late August seven separate lawsuits were filed in circuit court by creditors of the Bank of Macomb and the Bank of Colchester against the Chandlers and against Charles I. Imes, co-owner of the latter institution. On September 10, the creditor's committee met and agreed that an out-of-court settlement was no longer possible. The next day the U.S. District Court in Peoria appointed Blandinsville's Frank W. Brooks as receiver of the Chandler and Imes properties.[5]

The railroad was encountering its own problems while the fate of C.V. Chandler's financial empire was being wrangled over. In June service was suspended again due to rebuilding work on the perennially problematic Camp Creek Bridge. Just days later, on June 28, an injunction suit was filed in circuit court to prevent the M&WI from operating steam engines within the city of Macomb, or more specifically, near the residence of Maria Gamage.

Charles I. Imes, co-defendant in the civil suits against C.V. Chandler. Bateman & Shelby, The Historical Encyclopedia of Illinois and McDonough County.

The suit was filed by James W. Stuart, the same man who had successfully campaigned in court for the removal of the M&WI from Macomb, and included as co-sponsors five other members of the Gamage family, though they all later testified that they had not been involved with, or even been told about, the suit. The reason given was that Maria Gamage was in poor health, and the noise and smoke from the railroad's steam engines aggravated her condition. Master in Chancery Hampton heard the case on July 1, but before his decision came down Maria Gamage died and the case was dismissed.[6]

The railroad's problems continued. A Prairie City man sued the M&WI in August for $5,000 for injuries sustained in a horse runaway which he claimed was caused by the railroad's steam engine; this was settled out of court. St. Paul's Catholic Church's suit to have the tracks on Johnson Street fronting its property removed was settled in October; the railroad removed that half block's worth of tracks and paid the church $1 in damages.[7]

The saga of the Chandler bankruptcy continued through 1907 and into 1908. C.V. Chandler announced in late 1907 that he would not resist the bankruptcy, as he was sure he would be able to cover all of his debts in full. Frank W. Brooks was elected permanent receiver by Chandler's creditors the next month, and in January 1908, the first parcels of Chandler's properties, including the Hotel Chandler, the post office block, and the Macomb elevator, were put up for public auction.[8]

June 1, 1908, was the deadline set by the county court for the city of Macomb to force the removal of the M&WI's tracks within the city limits, and on that date, notice was served on the city council. A month later, on July 3, the railroad stopped operating its passenger trains up to Jackson Street, and instead terminated them at the Macomb Yards, just south of town. This provoked an uproar from the citizens living south of Macomb along the railroad, who were infuriated that a small group of people unhappy with the railroad had managed to go to court and force it off the streets of Macomb. Passenger traffic from the south fell off by two thirds due to the inconvenience of the new northern terminus.[9]

The Macomb business community, alarmed by the serious problems the M&WI was experiencing, was galvanized into action. Throughout June and July, the Macomb Commercial Association headed up efforts to find a new route for the railroad to use to get its passenger trains to downtown Macomb. C.V. Chandler, who no longer controlled the railroad but was still an expert on its operations, was a contributor to these meetings. Efforts focused on two options, both of which would result in a terminal being built about half a mile from the center of town. The first option was to build north starting from the fairgrounds on private right-of-way located between Johnson and McArthur Streets as far north as Chase Street, where a depot would be built. The second option was to build a branch from the railroad's current northern terminus at the West Sewerpipe Works along the south side of the Burlington as far east as either the Jackson Street or Carroll Street crossings. Chandler served as an unofficial representative of the railroad and also helped to temper the suggestions made. Some of the plans, including those to finally electrify the railroad, and others to extend it southward were extremely unrealistic considering the precarious nature of the railroad's finances. The first option, to build the railroad north to Chase Street, was soon abandoned as impossible. The second option, to construct tracks paralleling the CB&Q to the immediate south of that railroad's right-of-way, seemed practical but soon came up against insurmountable difficulties. In order to establish a swath of land wide enough to build its tracks, the M&WI would either have to condemn and tear down houses located along the south side of the CB&Q, which it could not afford to do, or buy a strip of land from the Burlington itself. The CB&Q flatly refused this proposal, and a counter-proposal it made to charge the M&WI for the right to have its trains hauled into downtown Macomb via the Burlington was turned down due to a variety of operational problems and concerns. The M&WI's trains would continue to terminate at the Macomb yards.[10]

C.V. Chandler's financial woes continued. Public sale of his properties in mid-1908 didn't raise nearly as much money as expected, and the sales of property owned by Chandler and the Bank of Macomb continued sporadically through 1908 and 1909. In late 1908 the question of whether the M&WI could be considered an asset of the Bank of Macomb came up. The railroad itself was not in bankruptcy, but the bank owned virtually all of the road's stock, and therefore it was determined that the railroad was indeed an asset of

This is the only surviving photo of the second M&WI steam engine numbered 1, a 4-4-0. It is posed, probably in the 1905-1908 period, with a mixed train consisting of a gondola, boxcar and combine 1 southbound at the Darius Runkle house just north of Littleton. This large house, built in 1866, was still standing in 2005. Image courtesy of the Schuyler County Jail Museum.

the bank. With this being the case, it was the job of Frank W. Brooks, as receiver, to convert the railroad into cash. That meant the M&WI was going to be sold.[11]

The first proposal to buy the railroad was made by its president, William A. Compton. He had been president of the railroad since its inception and was better acquainted with its operations than just about anyone. In October 1908, he submitted a contract to Brooks for an option, viable until February 1, 1909, to buy all of the stock and bonds of the M&WI owned by the bank for $125,000 (about $2.4 million in inflation-adjusted 2005 money). He also submitted his resignation as president of the M&WI, effective on February 1, 1909. Compton's proposal was regarded by the supporters of the railroad as the best hope for its continued survival, but they were to be disappointed. Compton was unable to raise the money he needed, and his effort collapsed. In early 1909 he was replaced as president of the railroad by Charles W. Flack.[12]

Charles W. Flack, who became the second president of the M&WI in early 1909. Bateman & Shelby, The Historical Encyclopedia of Illinois and McDonough County.

In February 1909, the Corn Exchange Bank of Chicago began pressuring Frank Brooks to find a buyer for the M&WI. The Bank of Macomb owned all of the stock of the railroad, but the Corn Exchange Bank owned $70,000 worth of the road's bonds and was considering foreclosing on the M&WI. It brought in a wrecking company to evaluate the railroad and determined that the scrap value of the property was about $70,000. Brooks, in an effort to gain complete control over the railroad, which was still mostly owned by the Bank of Macomb, began negotiating with the Corn Exchange Bank to buy out its stake in the M&WI. In April he was able to make a deal whereby he would acquire, as receiver of the Bank of Macomb, the remainder of the railroad's bonds in exchange for $20,000 and a piece of property in downtown Chicago owned by Chandler. The railroad was now firmly in the hands of Receiver Brooks and was still operating regularly. In fact, in December 1909 an agreement was finalized with the CB&Q which allowed M&WI trains to enter downtown Macomb over the Burlington's tracks, and for use of the Burlington's depot in return for regular fees. Now, once again, the M&WI had access to downtown Macomb.[13]

The Chandler bankruptcy was finally being wrapped up. The early predictions that C.V. Chandler would be able to cover his debts had turned out to be false. His last gesture, an effort to save his railroad by trying to persuade the creditors of the Bank of Macomb to take over ownership of the M&WI and operate it for profit, was unsuccessful. Property formerly belonging to Chandler was sold throughout 1909, and in January 1910, Chandler's homestead at the corner of Carroll and McArthur Streets in Macomb, his last piece of property except for the railroad, was sold at public auction. C.V. Chandler, once one of the richest men in town and a leading citizen of Macomb, now owned nothing but a burial plot in Macomb's Oakwood Cemetery. He moved to Indianapolis to live with his son, no longer to have any influence on the railroad, whose existence he had made possible. [14]

In August 1910, pursuant to an order by the special referee of the Chandler bankruptcy, Frank W. Brooks put up for sale all of the capital stock and bonds of the M&WI. During the initial bid period, which extended to September, the only bid submitted was rejected for lack of financing. In early 1911, several parties began to express interest in purchasing the railroad. Colonel J.M. Myers, who had made the 1910 bid, introduced a proposal in February to sell stock in a company which would purchase the M&WI and possibly extend it to Rushville

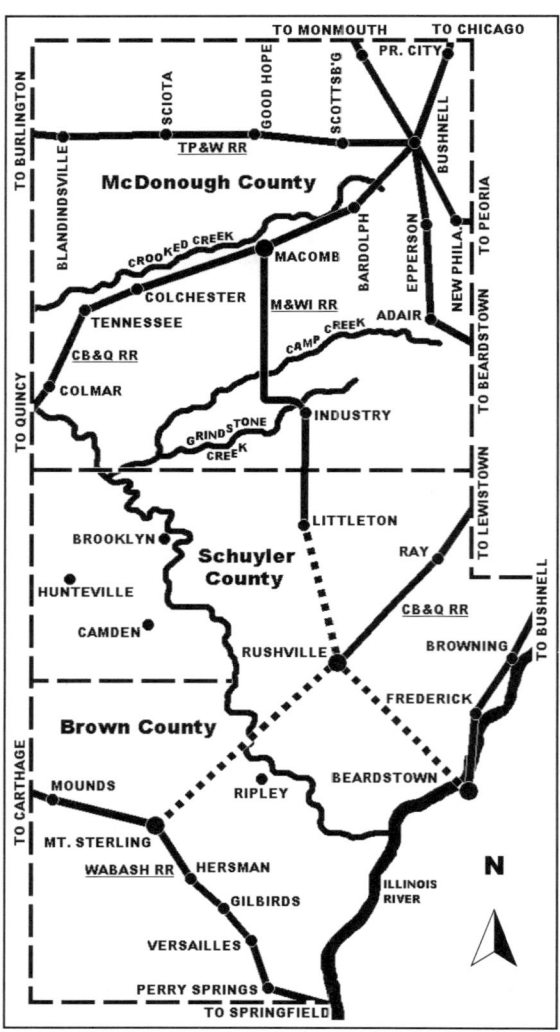

This map shows H.C. Billingsley's proposed expansion of the M&WI (dotted line). It would have made Rushville the junction of four railroad lines instead of the terminus of a minor branch of the CB&Q. Frank G. Hicks map.

and Mt. Sterling. This proposal soon collapsed. A more realistic, if undesirable, option was brought up in May, when a large scrapping company called Chicago House Wrecking (CHW) expressed a willingness to buy the M&WI for $25,000. At the end of May another auction date for the railroad was set by the special referee, this time in June. Again, no bids were accepted.

The possibility that the railroad might be sold for scrap prompted a number of people interested in saving the railroad to begin raising funds to buy the road. A man from Chicago, H.C. Billingsley, proposed in June that he would buy the M&WI for $100,000, raise $2 million from capitalists on the east coast, and use the new capital to electrify the railroad and extend it to Rushville, Beardstown, and Mt. Sterling. Few were willing to support such extravagant plans and his proposal was soon abandoned. A group of businessmen in Macomb led by Charles W. Flack and Isaac M. Fellheimer began raising money to buy the railroad, while a separate group of farmers and businessmen from Industry and Littleton, led by George N. Runkle and Thomas D. Sullivan, began canvassing for money for their own effort to purchase the road. As the *Macomb Daily Journal* put it, "There are so many propositions that one who aspires to become a magnate would be puzzled as to which proposition he should affiliate. There seems to be only one sure thing and that is that the future of the Macomb & Western Illinois railroad hangs in the balance."[15]

In late August 1911 the railroad was put on the auction block again, and this time there were two bidders. Chicago House Wrecking bid $30,000 for the entire property, while the group of Macomb businessmen bid $40,000. The bid by the Macomb businessmen undoubtedly saved the railroad from being sold for scrap at the time, but the bid was not actually accepted. Attorneys for the Bank of Macomb's creditors objected to the sale and asked for a thirty day extension on the bid period.[16]

On September 21, bids for the M&WI were due and no fewer than five bids were submitted for the railroad. Among these were bids for $40,000, submitted by the group of Macomb businessmen, a bid for $45,000 made by Fred Fitch, a capitalist from Kansas City, and another bid for $50,000 submitted by Chicago House Wrecking. What CHW did differently, though, was actually hand Frank W. Brooks a check for the sale amount on the day the bids were due, removing any doubt about its financial backing. That was all Brooks needed. He announced that the railroad had been sold to the wrecking company. Fitch appealed the sale in court, saying that CHW had acted improperly by submitting the purchase money along with its bid, and the case was heard in the U.S. Appeals Court in Chicago on January 4, 1912. Three weeks later, on January 23, the court found in favor of Frank Brooks. The sale to Chicago House Wrecking stood.[17]

This is one of the original M&WI gold bonds, issued in 1903, and signed by W.A. Compton and Ralph Chandler. Written over it in red ink is "Cancelled by deed of U.S. Court, Dec. 31, 1913" - the M&WI ceased to exist. WIU Special Collections

Men of Industry

With the sale of the M&WI, the bankruptcy of C.V. Chandler and Charles Imes was finally over. President Abe Harris of Chicago House Wrecking (CHW) paid Frank Brooks $50,000 for the railroad, as agreed upon, which enabled the creditors of the Chandler estate to see about sixty cents on the dollar for their initial investments. As for the railroad, its fate was not left to conjecture for long. Earlier vague claims by M&WI co-owners CHW and Chicago Assets Realization Company that they might extend, improve, or rebuild the M&WI were forgotten when on February 1, 1912, only a day after the sale, it was announced that the local managers of the "Little Road" had received instructions from Chicago that passenger service was to be suspended at once and that freight service was to last only one week longer. This was amended the same day on the advice of CHW attorneys, whose recommendation was that service continue one more week until CHW and M&WI officials had a chance to meet. Their advice was taken.[1]

Time was running out quickly for the railroad. On February 3, the state boiler inspector condemned the only operational steam engine, number 4, as unsafe. M&WI manager E.L. Tobie had a boiler inspector from Galesburg come the next day and reverse this judgment so that the railroad could continue

The intriguing photo above, of five men standing on the pilot beam of M&WI engine 4, is of uncertain vintage but may be a 1914 photo of some of the founders of the Macomb Industry & Littleton Railway. WIU Special Collections.

operating. On February 5, the CB&Q announced that its contract to interchange freight and passenger cars with the "Little Road" had expired with the transfer of ownership of the M&WI, and that it would no longer accept any M&WI cars on its rails. Tobie again came to the rescue, persuading the Burlington to allow freight cars to be switched between the two railroads, but passenger service had to be cut back to the Macomb Yards once again. A testy exchange between Macomb businessmen and the Burlington ensued, with the locals suggesting that the city government compel the CB&Q to accept M&WI trains.[2]

On February 13, it became a moot point. The axe fell when CHW suspended all freight and passenger service on the "Little Road" permanently. Passenger service ended with the last train that day, and within four days all interchange freight cars had been taken to the Burlington for transfer off the M&WI. CHW officials began work on closing the mail contract. In the meantime, they made other arrangements for hauling mail to Industry and Littleton.[3]

The reaction to the closure of rail service was an outpouring of support for continuation of operations. The same railroad, which for years had suffered through the complaints and lawsuits of a minority of the people it served, was now the subject of others' most strenuous efforts to keep it alive. On March 19, a month after service ended, the largest businessmen's meeting in years was held in Macomb. The purpose was to come up with a plan to not only save the M&WI by buying it back from the wrecking company, but to improve and expand it into a north-south connector like that which had been envisioned ten years earlier. E.L. Tobie was the primary force behind the movement to buy and extend the M&WI. His plan was to create a company called the St. Louis Macomb & Northern (SLM&N) which would be extended south to Rushville and north to a connection with the Atchison Topeka & Santa Fe, probably at Stronghurst. The amount of money necessary to build the railroad to modern standards, $1.2 million, was staggering, but Tobie believed $684,000 could be raised by a bond issue and $600,000 by selling capital stock.[4]

Reaction to this plan was enthusiastic. Tobie managed to convince many of the businessmen of Macomb, Raritan, Rushville, and Sciota of the merits of his plan. The people of Industry and Littleton, of course, were in support of anything that would save the railroad, which was their link to the rest of the country. On April 1, 1912, Mayor Keefer of Macomb became the first subscriber to the SLM&N bond issue with a purchase of $1,000, and by the end of the meeting that night at the Macomb Club, over $25,000 worth of bonds had been sold. Within two weeks, committees had been formed for each of the towns along the intended right-of-way to canvass the area for funding.[5]

The fundraising went slowly, but by late May 1912, Tobie was close to his goal of raising $600,000 for the bond issue. It took two extensions of the original May 1 deadline set by Chicago House Wrecking, but by June 18, the entire amount had been raised, $55,000 of it in the last two weeks of canvassing alone. Tobie went to Chicago to meet with the CHW representatives and on May 24, an agreement was signed with CHW to sell the "Little Road" to the SLM&N pending the securing of the entire right-of-way.[6]

The future of the M&WI remained uncertain. Ownership was still in the hands of Chicago House Wrecking, and it was now up to Tobie to accomplish two tasks. First, he needed to survey and purchase the land that would be needed to extend the M&WI north and south. Second, he had to secure the funds necessary to cover the remaining $600,000 needed to actually construct the extensions. Tobie first turned his attention to the surveying, which began in early July 1912. The route was easy for most of the distance, but on the north side of Macomb, Crooked Creek, later renamed the Lamoine River, created a difficult obstacle. Several proposals of where the railroad should cross Crooked Creek were made in July and August, but by September, surveying work north of Macomb was essentially done.[7]

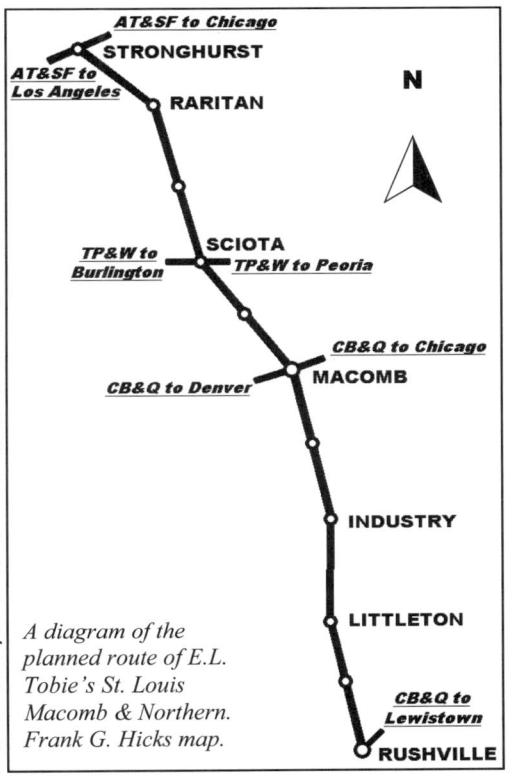

A diagram of the planned route of E.L. Tobie's St. Louis Macomb & Northern. Frank G. Hicks map.

Tobie next turned his attention to raising the additional $600,000. The communities around Macomb had been tapped for all of the money they could spare for the railroad, and it was obvious that outside investors would have to be brought in to construct the line to Stronghurst. For the first four months of 1913 Tobie spent his time trying to persuade financiers from Chicago to invest in the railroad, but by mid-May the wrecking company was getting impatient. With no evidence from Tobie that he would ever really be able to raise the additional funds that would be needed to build the SLM&N, the scrappers decided on May 17, 1913, to withdraw their offer to sell the railroad to Tobie and put its assets up for public sale. The grand effort to extend the M&WI had failed, and it was now up to the locals to save their railroad.[8]

Charles E. Nathan, a CHW representative, met with local leaders and agreed to give them some time to try and raise money to buy the railroad. A price of $90,000 was set. On May 22, 1913, Amos Ellis of Industry, and Van L. Hampton and Isaac M. Fellheimer of Macomb organized a meeting at the Macomb Club to formulate a plan to raise money among the local populace to

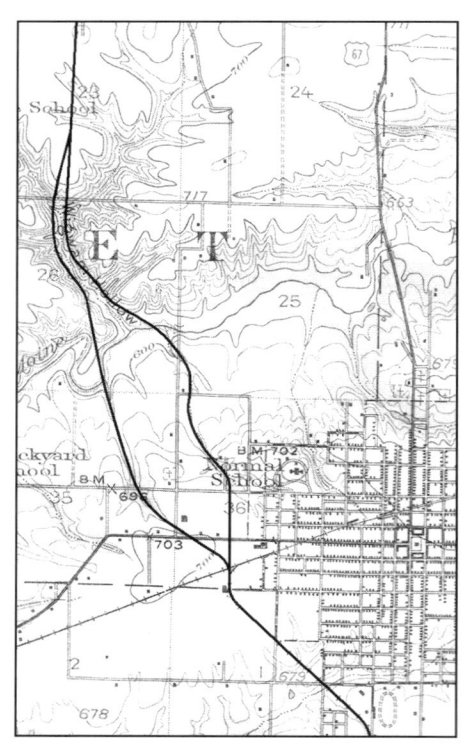

The two possible routes the SLM&N would have taken to cross Crooked Creek. Based on a 1912 U.S. Geological Survey map.

buy, repair, and operate the M&WI. A two-part proposal was forwarded to Chicago House Wrecking with a thirty day option. The committee offered to either purchase the M&WI for $55,000, or pay $25,000 for the right to lease and operate the railroad for a period of years to be agreed upon. This offer was swiftly rejected by CHW, which claimed it could get more than $55,000 by junking the railroad and $90,000 by selling its assets piecemeal.[9]

On May 27, there was another meeting to organize a movement to buy the "Little Road." More representatives from Littleton and Industry were present, with Frank Burnham, O.C. Gantz, and Robert and William Runkle offering reserved support. The next day I.M. Fellheimer and V.L. Hampton left for Chicago to meet with the owners of Chicago House Wrecking and Chicago Assets Realization Company. Their report, made in Macomb on June 2, was that they had secured an option to buy the railroad during the next forty-five days for $80,000. It was also said that Tobie still claimed that his financiers might yet pull through, and apparently this was regarded as the best hope for the project. By early August, though, it was clear that even an extension of the option was not going to be enough. The financiers from Chicago, Lansing, and Detroit who had been consulted had refused to contribute to the project, and the contract that had been drawn up was left unsigned. It was back to the drawing board.[10]

The real beginning of what would become the Macomb Industry & Littleton Railway took place during a meeting on August 7, 1913, at the M&WI office in Macomb. Isaac Fellheimer chaired the meeting. In attendance were James Little and Thomas Williams of Littleton, Frank Burnham, Oscar Gantz, John S. McGaughey, and William Kittering of the Doddsville area, and Amos and Forrest Ellis, Frank Hussey, and George W. Garrison representing Industry. The decision was made to finally cast aside any offers of financing from outside. This time the railroad would be bought and owned by the people of Macomb, Industry, and Littleton, not by a bank, and not by investors from Chicago. On August 12, there was another meeting, this time in

Industry, where a contract for a $100,000 stock subscription to purchase and rebuild the M&WI was presented. Thomas D. Sullivan of Industry moved to create an executive committee which would have charge of executing the contract and selling the stock. This committee consisted of James Little and J.D. Horton representing Littleton, Frank Burnham and John McGaughey of Doddsville, Tom Sullivan and Horace A. Hoffman of Industry, and Isaac Fellheimer and Van L. Hampton of Macomb.[11]

At first it appeared that this new movement presented a real hope to save the M&WI, but within a month it seemed that the end was at hand. "It looks as though the last move has been made and the 'Little Road'... is doomed to be wrecked, and that at once," reported the *Macomb Daily Journal* on September 15, 1913. Representatives from the wrecking company had arrived in Macomb to survey the M&WI, and arrange the repairs to the bridges and right-of-way that would be necessary to haul scrap metal over the railroad. A week later, on September 23, scrapping began at Littleton. Wrecking crews began tearing up the rails and loading them onto flatcars for transport to Chicago, while other crews repaired bridges to allow the locomotive to haul work trains from the Macomb Yards to the south end of the railroad where the scrapping work was going on. By the end of the month the water tower equipment in Littleton was pulled out and sold for scrap, the old wheeled scrapers still sitting in the Macomb Yards were sold for scrap, and the track wye at Littleton was removed. An appeal from Fellheimer and Hampton on behalf of the executive committee to delay the wrecking went unheeded by CHW. There was only one option left for the railroad's supporters, who were short on time and money. They had to go to court.[12]

The farmers who owned land along the railroad intended to fight the wrecking company using the Criminal Trespass Act. When the M&WI had been built by Chandler, much of the land for the railroad had essentially been given to the railroad on permanent loan, but it was to be used only for operation of the railroad. In the case the railroad was abandoned, title to the land would revert back to the original owner. Since CHW was not operating the railroad, but rather removing it for the purpose of scrap, the landowners argued that the reversion clause had been activated and the land, including the railroad tracks on it, was now theirs. J.D. Horton, a farmer living near Littleton, swore out arrest warrants against the scrapping company workers on October 1. A week later George Runkle followed suit.[13]

There was a also backup plan, in case the courts ruled that the wrecking company could use the railroad as long as the tracks were in place. George E. "Elsie" Garrison, a farmer living south of Macomb, owned a parcel of land which had been given over for use by the M&WI under a different arrangement. Rather than this parcel being promised to the M&WI for as long as the railroad was operating, then-landowner George Garrison (apparently "Elsie's" father) had given the land to the railroad only for the duration of his lifetime. He had since died, and although the railroad could have condemned his land through the usual eminent domain proceedings while it was operating, it hadn't, and it was no longer capable of doing so since it wasn't operating any more. On October 10, while CHW continued sending its workers south to Littleton to continue tearing up the railroad, "Elsie" Garrison swore out a warrant against the wrecking crew for trespassing.[14]

Efforts by CHW lawyers were unsuccessful in deterring Garrison. On October 13, Garrison had Engineer Thomas Williams, Foreman Lawrence Burke and Superintendent W.G. Bennett of the wrecking crew arrested and put in the Industry jail. A week later a jury of six men in Industry heard the case, and they found in favor of Garrison. Bennett was fined five dollars and the other two were fined two dollars and fifty cents each. With the court confirming that Garrison's land was indeed his, and that CHW could not move its workers across it at will, Garrison swore out warrants against ten other men who had also been on the scrapping crew.[15]

It worked. The scrapping halted while the CHW lawyers in Chicago decided how to handle the case. At the same time the movement to buy the railroad gained steam, and others, including William R. Clawson, Amos S. Ellis, George W. Garrison, John F. Lawyer, Charles W. Runkle, and Andrew E. Rush joined the effort. A meeting was held in the Women's Christian Temperance Union hall in Industry to bolster support for those fighting the wrecking company in court and to take further steps toward buying the railroad. It was decided to form a company to do this. The money collected by the committee thus far to buy the railroad would be transferred to the new company. A new executive committee of Frank Burnham, George Runkle, and A.E. Rush was formed.[16]

At the end of October the owners of the wrecking company threw the locals a curveball. Through a complex series of legal maneuvers they arranged to have a New Yorker named John W. McKinnon appointed the new trustee of the M&WI, replacing Continental Bank of Chicago, the old trustee. What this did was to throw the issue of ownership of the railroad into federal court rather than local court. Two days later Sangamon Loan & Trust, the receiver for the M&WI, asked that the U.S. District Court in Peoria order the rails, ties, and other railroad materials be torn up, and confirm that any interference be considered in contempt of court. Judge Humphreys gave this order, and scrapping resumed. The farmers did not give up so easily, however. "Elsie" Garrison swore out more warrants against the wrecking crew workers, and several farmers along the railroad built fences across the tracks to impede the southbound wrecking trains. The fences were unceremoniously run over, but by each evening most had been rebuilt and had to be run over again on the trip back north. George Runkle went so far as to build, and rebuild, this fencing himself so that none of his farmhands could be charged with contempt of court.[17]

"Elsie" Garrison's arrest warrants were executed on Halloween, 1913 by Constable John Lawyer of Industry, not to be confused with attorney John F. Lawyer, and the next day Industry's Justice of the Peace Ellis ruled that the U.S. District Court order did not give the scrapping company the right to destroy the farmers' property. That same day the scrapping company, through

Sangamon Loan & Trust, charged attorneys Charles Flack, John F. Lawyer, and T.B. Switzer, States Attorney Falder, Justice of the Peace Ellis, Constable Lawyer, and George "Elsie" Garrison with contempt of court.[18]

Judge Humphrey heard the case in Peoria on November 6, 1913. He ruled for the defendants, saying no contempt of court had occurred. However, he gave an opinion that if the question of reversion of property were to come before him, he would rule in favor of the wrecking company. Though he gave no official decision, it was his opinion that the scrapper had the right to tear up the railroad. The *Macomb Daily Journal* wrote that the railroad's supporters "see no reason for continuing the fight any longer. The price asked by the owners of the road is prohibitive, and there seems to be nothing left but to let it go."[19]

John F. Lawyer c1913. Bateman & Shelby, The Historical Encyclopedia of Illinois and McDonough County.

Four days later, however, their hopes were alive again. The three-man committee formed in October had been in negotiations with W.G. Bennett of Chicago House Wrecking and came to an agreement to purchase the railroad for $68,000, with a nonrefundable $1,000 down payment to be made within a week. But miscommunications between the owners of the railroad sank the deal. Edward Ridgley, who was owner of Chicago Assets Realization Company and co-owner of the railroad along with CHW, refused to give his permission to accept the offer for $68,000. Negotiations continued in an on-again, off-again manner during much of November. The *Macomb Daily Journal* wrote "Like Banquo's ghost, the Macomb and Western Illinois railroad will not down [sic], but rises in some form or another continuously." And so it was that on November 25, 1913, an agreement acceptable to all parties was reached between the local committee and the wrecking company. The committee bought the M&WI for $70,000 (adjusted for inflation, about $1.3 million in 2005 dollars), with the option extending until December 28, and guaranteed by a $1,000 forfeit paid every ten days until then. Half of the purchase price would be made in cash, half in "acceptable notes." Subscriptions made previously to Tobie's St. Louis Macomb & Northern would be returned immediately to avoid claims of misuse, and a new company would be organized to acquire the railroad with $100,000 of capital stock.[20]

On November 26, 1913, a meeting was held at Industry to consider the financial aspects of the venture. Two days later the contract was signed

> We had a railroad. Remember the M. I. & L.? It had its troubles and plenty of them. I was secretary of this road for seven years and am very familiar with its ups and downs, mostly down. This road was first operated in 1904, went into bankruptcy in 1911, and taken over by local farmers and businessmen in 1913, and died very dead in 1928. I could tell a lot of stories about this railroad, so many they would make a book. One I will relate is how near some of us came to getting in jail for contempt of the U.S. court. The road was in bankruptcy and was sold to the Chicago Wrecking Company. At the same time local men were working frantically to raise money to buy the road and get it going again. The wrecking company was going to start tearing up the road. In order to gain time in raising funds, some of the less timid would take up a rail or two, pile obstructions on the track so as to slow up the wrecking. This didn't set well with the wrecking company so they complained to the Federal judge in Peoria who called the obstructionists before him and threatened to jail every man that interfered. Some said he had a twinkle in his eye and was not very severe. Soon after the money was raised and the new company was organized.
>
> *Recollections of Horace Hoffman, from notes for a 1948 speech to the Kiwanis Club.*

and the work of canvassing the countryside for funds began. It wouldn't be easy. Although Tobie had been able to raise over half a million dollars for his railroad, there was a marked difference between the well-built connecting railroad he had proposed and the run-down stub short line that the new committee planned to acquire and put into operation again. The M&WI would need extensive rebuilding. The scrapping crews had removed the rails as far north as the county line, and the railroad's locomotives and rolling stock were in abysmal condition. Fundraising was very successful toward the south end of the line, where the M&WI had been the primary link between the communities of Littleton and Industry and the outside world, but interest in Macomb was virtually nonexistent. By the second week of December, Macomb, with a population about twice that of the Industry and Littleton areas combined, had contributed only $18,000 of the $67,000 raised thus far. By mid-December, with a majority of the capital stock subscribed to, an organizing meeting was called. On December 18, a notice appeared in the newspaper calling for all subscribers to the capital stock of the Macomb Industry & Littleton Railway to attend the organizing meeting at the Industry Opera House on December 23. The notice was signed by George N. Runkle, Frank Burnham, Andrew E. Rush, Thomas D. Sullivan, and James Little, Directors and Incorporators.[21]

The meeting on December 23 was the culmination of nearly two years of strenuous effort on the part of hundreds of people to save the little railroad that C.V. Chandler had built. Beleaguered during its operating lifetime of only nine years, the M&WI had still been a tremendous boon to the communities and the people it served. They had stood by while its future was determined during the Chandler bankruptcy, but once its fate seemed sealed, they had been galvanized into action. These men of Industry and Littleton had displayed a determination, enterprise, and industriousness in the face of unlikely odds and regrettable misfortunes that had finally paid off. The *Industry News* described what happened at the organizing meeting when it became obvious that the

One of the shares of capital stock in MI&L, this gold-toned certificate for share number 153 was owned by Eva Colby. WIU Special Collections.

committee was $8,000 short of the funds needed to buy the M&WI: "At the meeting Tuesday G.N. Runkle and W.R. Clawson rose and stated they would add $2,000 each to their subscriptions providing they could raise $4,000 more in the crowd. Calvin Wilson responded by raising the subscription of his father, J. Wilson, $1,000, and was quickly followed by others, $5,000 being raised inside of five minutes' time." The next day, collection began on the subscription money, and on December 28, the new company's directors left for Chicago along with Attorneys Flack and Lawyer to finalize the purchase. On December 30, 1913 the deal was struck. The "Little Road" now belonged to the Macomb Industry & Littleton Railway Company.[22]

Strides of Progress

They had done it. The men to whom the "Little Road" meant the most, the farmers and businessmen of southern McDonough and northern Schuyler counties, had saved the railroad themselves. No longer would the line's patrons have to sit by and watch while the fate of the railroad was decided in the courts of Macomb and Peoria. Now the customers became the owners.

The euphoria of those who had worked so hard and so long to save the Macomb Industry & Littleton (MI&L), as it would now be known, was likely short lived. The railroad they had bought was a shambles. With the loss of the trackage rights agreement that had allowed M&WI trains to enter downtown Macomb along the Burlington, the line had lost its northern passenger terminal, and the scrapping crews of Chicago House Wrecking had torn up the southern three miles of the railroad entirely, cutting it back to about the McDonough-Schuyler county line. The condition of the track that was still in place was abysmal in many spots. Some of the bridges had been only temporarily fixed by the scrapping company to allow for the wrecking trains, and the overall condition of the roadbed was not safe enough to attempt passenger service. The rolling stock of the railroad was also little better than junk, having gone through months or years of deferred maintenance and disuse.[1]

The initial meeting of the MI&L directors following the sale of the railroad was on January 1, 1914, in Industry. Those officials who came from Macomb took the train, naturally, using the occasion to inspect the northern half of the railroad. They were accompanied by William Hendrickson and Jack O. Moon, both of whom had experience in railroad construction. The line was judged to be in reasonable shape considering its history, and the railroad

The only steam engine the railroad ever bought new was the attractive 2-6-0 Mogul shown above, built by Davenport Locomotive Works in 1914. WIU Special Collections.

officials coming from the north made it to the Industry meeting to participate in the discussions of how to conduct repairs of the railroad. The trip back, though, was a different matter. Badly leaking flues on the line's only operational steam engine, number 4, meant it kept losing steam pressure, and therefore, traction. After a series of starts and stops to build up pressure it failed utterly to push the combine, in which the railroad officials were riding, up the north side of the Troublesome Creek depression. An effort was made to get the combine across the shallow valley by uncoupling it on the south rise and letting it coast up the other side, but the brakes on the car didn't work and Charles Runkle managed to tumble down the railroad's embankment during an attempt to arrest the free-rolling combine. The dead steam engine and combine were left at the bridge and the directors had to walk the last three miles back to Macomb in a blinding snow storm, not arriving home until 9:00 at night. It wasn't until the next day that water could be carried out to the steam engine to raise steam, and bring it back to the Macomb Yards under its own power.[2]

No sooner had the MI&L been saved from an untimely death than E.L. Tobie, the author of the ill-fated 1912 plan to buy and extend the railroad, approached the directors with yet another scheme. This time he proposed bringing in a railroad construction manager from Lansing, Michigan, named W.T. McCaskey to help rebuild the line. The arrangement would involve McCaskey being paid $25,000, half in cash and half in stock, to rebuild the MI&L. The catch was that McCaskey would also be represented on the board of directors and would have a say in who managed the road, most likely to be Mr. Tobie. The MI&L directors, having just managed to secure the railroad's future in the hands of interested locals, were wary of someone from outside of Illinois, someone motivated more by profit than by any interest in providing service to McDonough and Schuyler counties, having a say in the development of the MI&L, and they refused the offer.[3]

That did not prevent the rebuilding of the MI&L, but it took a little longer to raise additional funds to pay for the construction. Jack Moon was placed in charge of the track and bridge work that commenced the second week of January after the steam engine's flues were replaced, and work soon commenced on the biggest headache on the line, the Camp Creek Bridge. G.W. Rollett, a Burlington manager who had supervised the construction of the CB&Q depot in Macomb the previous year, was employed as General Manager in late January and he brought in an experienced bridge repair engineer from the Burlington to help direct operations at Camp Creek. By the end of the month, repairs to the railroad had been completed as far south as Camp Creek, and during a directors' meeting on February 3, station agents were hired. O. Sweazy regained his agency in Macomb, Fred Duncan became the Industry agent, and Kohn Little was hired to staff the Littleton depot.[4]

Freight service on the MI&L commenced for the first time on February 8, 1914, with the opening of the Camp Creek Bridge, and reestablishment of rail service between Macomb and Industry. The railroad was still having problems with engine 4, and it needed a running start to make it up the

MI&L 4-4-0 locomotive 6, formerly of the Vandalia Railroad, shown hauling a mixed train southbound at Industry. WIU Special Collections.

grade on the south side of Camp Creek. Although the motive power problem would remain for the time being, other improvements were being made. The Industry depot opened with rebuilt stockyards, new freight rates had been established, and a movement was underway to relocate the Kirkpatrick switch to a point half a mile north of its former location.[5]

Freight service was lively during the first few weeks of renewed operation, but the acid test for the MI&L would be passenger service. It would not be easy to maintain a consistent schedule. With only one working steam engine, number 4, operation of all trains depended on the ability of that single locomotive to remain operational all of the time. Service would also be truncated: the northern end of the line terminated at the fairgrounds south of Macomb, and the southernmost stop was at the Runkle Switch, as the track south of there had been torn up by the wrecking crews. By the last week of February, impatient people eager to take the train had resorted to riding in boxcars, but on February 27, the MI&L finally instituted passenger service. It was "once more a full-fledged railroad with a passenger and freight service, and will run just as near on time as the average road," trumpeted the *Macomb Daily Journal*. Initially there were two round-trips daily. The southbound trains left Macomb at 8:30 a.m. and 3:30 p.m. and the northbound trains left Runkle at 10:45 a.m. and 4:40 p.m. The morning trains, likely scheduled mixed trains hauling both passengers and freight cars, had running times of about one hour forty-five minutes each way, but the afternoon trains cut that time down to about an hour.[6]

The arrival of a new steam engine, number 5, on April 22, 1914 heralded a new, more stable, more prosperous era for the MI&L. It was the first, and last, steam engine ever bought new by the "Little Road" and was built specially for short line passenger and freight service by the Davenport Locomotive Works located just seventy-five miles to the north. Only a week later, the MI&L finally returned to Littleton. Manager Rollett's crews hadn't stopped working after completion of the Camp Creek Bridge but had continued southward, laying down rails on the roadbed in Schuyler County to replace track that had been torn up by Chicago House Wrecking just six months before. The work was hard and not always safe. In late March, a handcar traveling toward Macomb was derailed at the edge of town by a brick wedged in the flangeway at a crossing, probably by a mischievous youngster. One of the section men was thrown from the handcar and injured. The work continued, however, and within two days after the railroad was completed to Littleton the track crews were at work widening the Kirkpatrick curve west of Industry, from fourteen to eight degrees, to allow for higher speeds and safer operation. Passenger operation into Littleton commenced as soon as the track was laid, and on April 29, 1914, a timetable was issued that would remain in effect for the next five years. Northbound trains left Littleton at 6:50 a.m. and 11:45 a.m. and arrived at the Macomb Yards, south of town, at 8:10 a.m. and 1:15 p.m. respectively. Southbound trains left Macomb at 9:00 a.m. and 4:00 p.m., arriving at Littleton at 10:30 a.m. and 5:30 p.m. The trains were numbered, with trains 1 and 3 completing northbound passenger runs, and trains 2 and 4 making southbound runs.[7]

In March 1915, an agreement was finalized with the CB&Q that allowed the passenger trains of the MI&L to access downtown Macomb. It was similar to the old 1908 agreement. The MI&L would use the Burlington's depot and ticket agent for an annual fee of $324, it would pay the Burlington two dollars per car for each round trip between the MI&L interchange and the depot, or two dollars in each direction for each loaded freight car (empty freight cars were to be handled free), and it would pay the Burlington twenty cents per ton for all freight that passed through the Macomb depot.[8]

A week after the trackage rights agreement with the Burlington was re-established, MI&L engineer Alphonse Woerly left for Terre Haute, Indiana, to pick up a newly-purchased steam engine. Vandalia Railroad 302, soon to become MI&L 6, was another 4-4-0 American type engine, similar to, but larger and newer than the worn out and unserviceable number 4. While Woerly was on his trip, the need for another reliable engine was made obvious. The specter of suspension of service rose again as engine 5 broke two staybolts, sidelining it, and halting passenger and freight for a day. Traffic resumed when the Vandalia Railroad locomotive arrived and was immediately put into service.[9]

With terminals in Littleton and in downtown Macomb established, and with sufficient motive power to effectively maintain service, the MI&L had finally reached a point of equilibrium. The successful and relatively prosperous times which the MI&L experienced in the late teens saw relatively little change in the operations of the company. The company suffered a blow on

> ### A Ride on the MI&L
> Well Grandpa got acquainted with the people that were on the MI&L and so one day he said "I'd like to take a trip with you." And they said "Well, bring your lunch and come ahead." Now they had two or three freight cars and one or two passenger cars – depending on what they were expecting – and it started there on the west side of Lafayette Square, there was the little depot. Now sometimes they made just one trip down and back, sometimes they made two trips in a day, depending upon what was happening – sometimes according to crops and things like that. Well we had these children that lived in our neighborhood whose father worked at the factory – we knew they didn't have much. And then we had lemonade stands, and we'd make money and we'd buy clothes for those kids for the next year. If the circus came to town, we always bought the circus tickets for all of us. Well, then we decided one year we wanted to go on a picnic, and Grandpa suggested that he would go with us and he would make arrangements that we could all go on the MI&L to Littleton. And we got on the train that morning and the conductor shook hands with everyone very graciously and did everything he could to make us feel happy and told us he would come back and get us at different times and take us up to the engine so that everyone would be certain to be in the engine. By the time we got back and he suggested if we could have a boy and a girl at a time that was better, well we all got up there and Grandpa, of course, was with us supervising. We stopped at, always, someplace before we got to Industry for 15, 20 minutes and we'd get off the train and run around a little bit and get back on. And when we got to Industry they'd say "Now we have a half hour here, you can walk downtown and back, but don't take your lunches off the train – you're not going to eat here." And we would go downtown, maybe we'd get a stick of gum or something, or if people knew someone there we might stop to see someone. And we'd come back to the train – they'd blow the whistle two or three times to tell us to start back. When we got down to Littleton there was a little park, just real close. Well the conductor and the brakeman and fireman would all take their lunches and go over; there was a well there that had real cold, good water, and they'd go over and eat with us and we'd play games. Then they'd load up, and if they had things we could help them load, they would let us help load, you know – they made you a part of it, so that the kids felt like they really had done something. And we came back to Industry, and had a period of time there, and then came on to Macomb.
> *Recollections of Viletta Hillery, excerpted from a November 16, 2004, interview.*

August 8, 1918, when fire engulfed a sizeable portion of downtown Industry. Six commercial buildings on the north side of Main Street, including the new Lindsey Theater and the building in which the MI&L offices were located, caught fire in the early hours of the morning, and burned to the ground despite the efforts of the town's population to extinguish the blaze. The MI&L offices, on the second floor of the Conger Building, were completely destroyed. The only salvageable documents were those inside the safe, which was found buried in smoldering rubble in the building's basement after the fire.[10]

The railroad did not stagnate, though. Improvements were being made and others contemplated. A secondhand combine was purchased in April 1920 from the Beaver Penrose & Northern Railroad in Colorado. It arrived late in May, and went into service after being repainted and refurbished. In September and October of 1920, a series of letters was exchanged between repre-

> **RAILWAY MOTOR CAR COMPANY OF AMERICA**
>
> MANUFACTURERS OF
> UNIT PASSENGER CARS
> COMBINATION, INSPECTION,
> SECTION, TRACK REPAIR CARS
> AND LOCOMOTIVES.
> OPERATED BY
> KEROSENE OR DISTILLATE
>
> GENERAL OFFICES:
> ❦ CHICAGO ❦
> 714 WESTMINSTER BUILDING
> Telephones: Randolph 5457-5458
>
> FACTORY:
> HAMMOND, INDIANA
> Telephone: Hammond 44
>
> **HAMMOND, IND.**
>
> #2 A. E. R.
>
> We do not care to negotiate any farther if it is the
> habit of the community to be suspicious of ca Company
> of our standing. Unless there is a spirit of cooperation
> and a desire on the part of the citizens it would not
> be a profitable place for us to be and certainly a poor
> place for us to invest.

An excerpt from a 1920 letter from the Railway Motor Car Company of America to A.E. Rush, President of the MI&L. WIU Special Collections.

sentatives from the MI&L and the Railway Motor Car Company of America, a fledgling builder of gasoline-powered locomotives and motorcars from Hammond, Indiana, regarding the possibility of RMCCA moving its plant to Macomb. Had an agreement been made, MI&L operations might have been revolutionized. RMCCA was willing to allow the MI&L to use its motorcars to hold down passenger service in exchange for permission to test its products on the line to Littleton prior to delivery. Both sides were justifiably suspicious of the others' stability. RMCCA is not thought to have ever actually gone into production of any full-size railway equipment. Needless to say, the deal fell through. Three years later, in January 1924, the possibility of using internal combustion came up again. Internal combustion locomotives had come a long way since the dubiously useful boxcab that the M&WI had bought in 1903. General Electric had already built a few prototype switching engines, and later in 1924, GE and Ingersoll-Rand debuted their successful line of 300 horsepower diesel-electric switchers. The *Macomb Daily Journal* reported that the MI&L officials prophetically believed that internal combustion "will eventually displace steam power;" but the finances of the railroad didn't allow for large capital investments in such modern equipment, and the purchase of an internal combustion locomotive was put off indefinitely. Thought was still being given to extending the MI&L, even at this late date. In 1922 an effort was made to raise interest in building an extension from Littleton to Camden, a distance of about twelve miles, but this came to naught.[11]

The busy and stable, if not particularly prosperous, years that the MI&L had enjoyed in the late teens and early 1920s were coming to an end. Times were changing, and with the coming of the automobile, the role of short lines like the MI&L was fast disappearing. During the early 1920s, freight and traffic levels on the railroad declined, and by the end of 1924, the MI&L was operating in the red. The hope appeared to lie in, ironically, the construction of hard roads. The State of Illinois was constructing several north-south main arteries, all of them paved and designed for automobile use. Illinois Route 3 (later US Route 67) would pass through Macomb and Industry and just to the east of Littleton, approximately paralleling the MI&L, and the construction companies bidding on the sections of the hard road south of Macomb promised large contracts to the "Little Road" in hauling gravel, cement, and other construction materials.[12]

But the year 1925, during which most of the construction of the Illinois Route 3 hard road between Macomb and Rushville took place, would not turn out to be the boon that the MI&L had hoped for. Over the course of the summer the railroad hauled train after train of construction materials south to Industry and Littleton, but for as much money as was coming in, more still was going out to keep the railroad running. The railroad to Littleton had been lightly built in 1903, and had never been significantly upgraded. Ballasting in most areas was poor or nonexistent, ties were of low quality, and the weight of the rail was mostly 56# (fifty-six pounds per yard), far lighter than the 80# or 90# rail used on larger railroads like the Burlington. The lighter rail fared well only when lightweight passenger cars or grain cars traversed the track. Conversely, when larger, modern freight cars loaded with gravel and other heavy materials traveled over the railroad repeatedly, they severely damaged the track. Reconstruction of the right of way ate up the profits from the haulage of hard road materials in 1925, and the general decline in traffic, both freight and passenger, combined with that loss to throw the MI&L $20,000 into debt by September.[13]

The crisis was serious. Operations continued normally through the fall, but expenses were cut to the bone to eliminate the operating deficit. The matter of how to erase the debt, though, was a difficult question. Some had argued earlier in the year that the downturn in business was only temporary, but whether temporary or permanent, the railroad's poor financial condition made it impossible for the MI&L to raise $20,000 through operating profit. At a meeting of the stockholders in November, a bond issue was debated and voted down. When that failed, A.E. Rush was appointed to chair a committee to investigate ways to pay down the debt. Frank B. Burnham, W.C. Butcher, J.W. Campbell, Charles O. Foulke,

Scenes like this, of Route 41 construction in Bushnell, were common along the MI&L in the 1920s as hard roads were built. WIU Special Collections.

Horace Hoffman, and Thomas D. Sullivan made up the committee. Their decision, presented at the annual meeting in January 1926, was to sell several parcels of land owned by the MI&L to pay off the debt. This land, which made up about seventy acres near Industry and Macomb plus several lots in Macomb itself, was sold in June 1926, and raised about $15,000. Other steps were also being taken to cut costs. In mid-November 1925, the MI&L petitioned the Interstate Commerce Commission to abandon two of its runs. Now, instead of two daily round trips between Macomb and Littleton, there would be only one; a morning run from Littleton to Macomb, and a return trip in the late afternoon.[14]

The relief afforded by the sale of land in 1926 was only temporary. The debt remained at about $5,000 after the sale, and during the year and a half following the property sale, the MI&L lost yet more money. Operation of trains became irregular, the contract to carry mail was given to a bus company, the company was unable to pay its taxes, and new stockyards in Bushnell halved the amount of stock the road carried. The year 1928 would prove to be a pivotal one for the "Little Road." At the beginning of the year, plans were unveiled to issue $25,000 worth of bonds to eliminate the debt and repair the right-of-way and equipment. The need for these bonds became apparent in late spring, at the same time the ICC approved the bond issue. A.C. Anders, the railroad's general manager since 1919, resigned in early May, and a Chicagoan named P.L. Elder was hired to replace him. Coincident with this was the cessation on May 10, 1928, of all operations. The reason was the need to overhaul the railroad's remaining operational steam engine, and the lack of the $3,000 needed to do it. In early June efforts to sell the bonds commenced, led by O.G. Gantz of Industry and A.J. Fish of Macomb. Time was short, as the contract to build the hard road from Littleton west to Brooklyn was to be let in June, and the MI&L was pinning its hopes for operational profits on haulage of materials for that project. But public reaction to the bond issue was discouraging. The people living along the railroad grew tired of the railroad's perennial problems, and they were unimpressed by projections of $40,000 projected gross income from the Littleton hard road business and of the railroad being self-sustaining within the year. On June 22, 1928, the Board of Directors of the MI&L voted to abandon the railroad and sell it for scrap.[15]

The announcement's effect was electrifying. The apparent impending death of the "Little Road" merited a full-width front page headline in the *Macomb Daily Journal*, and it impressed the people living along the line like nothing the canvassers had said. The justification for this drastic step was dif-

Headline from the June 23, 1928, issue of the Macomb Daily Journal.

ficult to controvert. The railroad was $15,000 in debt, and its assets were unlikely to be worth much more than $20,000. No trains had operated in over six weeks, and unless $3,000 could be raised to repair one of the steam engines, operations could not be resumed. That was money the MI&L simply did not have. It had been depending on the citizens living along the line to put $25,000 toward the railroad to keep it operating, but they had declined. The railroad had run out of options.[16]

Whether the MI&L directors actually intended to scrap the railroad or not is conjecture. In all likelihood they were perfectly willing to, considering the business outlook. But it did not come to pass. Following the announcement of the decision to abandon the railroad, money began coming in to buy the bonds the MI&L had issued. The railroad was still extremely important to the farmers living along the line, who used it regularly to ship livestock and grain, and it was vital to the contractors building the hard road out of Littleton, who had set their bid price on the project with the ability to haul materials from the CB&Q to Littleton via the MI&L in mind. Within six weeks the entire $25,000 bond issue had been subscribed to, repairs were underway, and operations were set to begin. General Manager Elder was fired and replaced by F.B. McPeek, who would later be succeeded by the same A.C. Anders who had resigned the previous May. Freight and passenger operations finally resumed in August, and starting in September the MI&L was back hauling hard road materials to Littleton.[17]

The temporary infusion of cash did not save the railroad as promised. The decline in the railroad's fortunes was not a temporary blip, it was a trend reflected in the fortunes of interurbans and short line railroads across the country in the late 1920s. As the nation's network of paved roads spread and automobile ownership exploded, the need for short-haul railroads like the MI&L declined dramatically. Within six months of the bond sale, it became apparent that the railroad's fortunes were not improving. Operation of the elevator in Littleton ceased in June in anticipation of the MI&L shutting down. In July, the elevator was leased to H.L. Mummert, manager of the Industry elevator and an MI&L director, and reopened. Hauling of hard road materials to Littleton continued into the summer until that project ended, and during the late summer harvest season, the MI&L was kept busy hauling bumper crops of oats and wheat.[18]

The final straw came in September 1929. On September 23, the Great Lakes Coal & Coke Company, which supplied the coal to keep the "Little Road's" steam engine running, filed suit against the MI&L for $528.70 in unpaid coal bills. The line's locomotive was attached, or seized, and towed to a Burlington siding under the observation of Sheriff Paul Eakle. About two weeks later the Union National Bank, acting on behalf of the MI&L as a trustee, settled with Great Lakes Coal & Coke and the engine was returned, but the lesson was clear. The railroad was in a shambles. The locomotive was on its last legs, most of the rolling stock was barely operational, and some bridges and portions of the right-of-way had been condemned by railroad safety inspectors. On October 8, 1929, a delegation consisting of MI&L directors William R. Clawson, V.A. Horney, H.L. Mummert, and Eli Willey, and attorney Myron Mills went to Springfield to ask permission to petition the Illinois Commerce Commission to authorize abandonment of the MI&L. Horney summed it up, stating "While the railroad will be greatly missed by Littleton and Industry, the need for this service has diminished considerably in the past few years with the building of hard roads through this territory."[19]

Just days after the petition was filed, the Moline Construction Company filed suit against the MI&L for foreclosure. Charles E. Flack, a Macomb attorney, was appointed receiver in late 1929. Another nail in the MI&L's coffin came on January 17, 1930, when the Union National Bank of Macomb filed a foreclosure suit of its own. On February 5, after hearing Charles Flack's argument advocating abandonment of the MI&L, Circuit Court Judge George C. Hillyer signed the order authorizing the railroad to petition the ICC for permission to abandon and scrap the railroad. The railroad was still running trains sporadically, but operations ended at the end of March when the decision of the ICC came down. Permission to abandon the Macomb Industry & Littleton was granted. The life of the railroad that had been built by C.V. Chandler, that had been saved by farmers and businessmen, that had been owned its entire operating life by the people of McDonough and Schuyler counties, was over.[20]

Disposition of the railroad did not take long. The entire property of the railroad, including all of the track, rolling stock, buildings, and land, was put up for auction on May 1, 1930 and sold to the highest bidder. The sale of the railroad and the various parcels of land totaled $20,370.50. The largest parcel, consisting of all of the rails, locomotives, and rolling stock, was bought by D.A. Harper of Galesburg for $17,550. The railroad's obituary was printed in the May 5, 1930 *Macomb Daily Journal* under the headline "MI&L Railroad

MI&L 5 is shown back at its birthplace in Davenport for scheduled heavy maintenance and inspection work in 1925. WIU Special Collections.

The only known photo of engine 5 in actual use is this one, taken near the end of service on the MI&L. Otis Gunning is the engineer and Joseph Johnson the fireman. Schuyler County Jail Museum, Schuyler County: Illinois History.

Crowded Out by the Strides of Progress, Once the Hope of Entire Countryside." It was a fitting tribute to a venture which had formerly been so important in the lives of the people and communities it served, yet which had been rendered obsolete and unnecessary. The work of scrapping the MI&L began in Littleton on May 20, and by the end of the month the Briggs-Turving Wrecking Company had progressed past the point at which Chicago House Wrecking had halted its demolition in 1913. The railroad was torn up as far north as Industry by the second week of June. By June 19, the railroad had been removed as far as the Macomb Yards, and the fleet of freight cars had been burned, with the metal parts hauled away for scrap. On June 23, 1930, it was all over. The last rails were taken up on the west side of town, the two passenger cars sold for use as hog sheds, and the steam engine hauled dead to Galesburg for rebuilding and resale. The *Macomb Daily Journal's* account concluded, "Thus ends the history of the 'Little Road.'"[21]

Afterword

On September 17, 1929, a quarter of Macomb's population of 10,000 gathered in Chandler Park to dedicate a memorial to the man who had worked harder for the good of Macomb than any other. C.V. Chandler, who for nearly two decades had been living in Indianapolis, came back to his hometown to attend the unveiling of a memorial arch in the park he had created. At 87 years of age, the old man was treated to an emotional day of receptions, dinners, and reminiscences with the grateful citizens of Macomb.

Only a few short miles away, on the southern edge of town, the railroad that Chandler had made possible, the railroad that had been of so much benefit to Macomb and the territories south of the city, the railroad that had been the ultimate cause of Chandler's bankruptcy and disgrace back in 1910, was in the last stages of its slow, terminal decline. Its last decrepit engine still made occasional forays to Littleton and Industry over rollercoaster track and condemned bridges, but it was obvious to all involved that the MI&L was at the precipice of extinction. Within six months of the dedication of the memorial arch to C.V. Chandler, the railroad so closely associated with that man, would be abandoned. Within twelve it would be gone.

There are not many traces of the Macomb Industry & Littleton left today. The men who built and ran the railroad died off gradually. George N. Runkle died in 1928, Frank Brooks survived the line by only months, dying in May 1930. C.V. Chandler died in 1934, Charles Flack in 1950, and William A. Compton in 1955. James Ira Hodges, the engineer who had been injured in the Industry wreck in 1907, survived into the 1970s. The tracks were all torn up and most of the buildings razed soon after the railroad stopped operating. The elevators in Littleton and Industry were torn down, replaced by newer structures, while the elevators built between towns disappeared. The Littleton depot survived until it was destroyed by a tornado in 1981. There are no other buildings from the railroad known for certain to survive. Structures exist on Lafayette Street in Macomb and at the Runkle Switch site that resemble railroad buildings, but their heritage cannot be definitely determined. Grading for the railroad is still evident in several places, particularly on the northwest side of Industry where the grade over Grindstone Creek is quite obvious. It's also apparent on the north side of Littleton, where the large concrete culvert that carried the MI&L over Sugar Creek still stands and the right of way at that point is used for an access road.

The effects that the railroad had on the towns and people it served were, perhaps, longer lasting. It is impossible to determine how much wealth the railroad brought the merchants of Macomb by carrying in shoppers from the south, how much money the farmers between Macomb and Littleton were able to save by having a convenient means of transporting goods close at hand, or how much the communities of Industry and Littleton benefited from being connected to the national railroad network. The MI&L served an important purpose during the years it existed, and it was eventually cast aside for a more modern means of accomplishing the same. The railroad was never directly replaced, though, and Industry and Littleton never truly regained their unusual status as focal points for local trade and traffic. Route 67 may carry far more people and freight than the MI&L ever did, but no one driving at 40 miles per hour through Industry spends a few minutes running over to the corner drug store to buy a stick of gum. No one speeding by a mile east of Littleton takes an hour to have a picnic in the park or ponders staying the night in town.

The "Little Road" that was once so important to the towns of Macomb, Industry, and Littleton vanished along with a way of life, but it is worth remembering how much the railroad meant to the people and communities that thrived along its tracks.

The potbelly stove from the MI&L Littleton depot is displayed at the Schuyler County Jail Museum.

This concrete culvert remains on the north side of Littleton, carrying the MI&L right-of-way over Sugar Creek. Frank Hicks photographs.

Appendix A
Trackage and Structures

The route of the MI&L remained fairly constant for its entire life with the exception of trackage north of the Macomb Yards; unfortunately documentation is still not entirely complete. Questions remain about specifics regarding the track and structures owned by the railroad, but these will be addressed in this account.

Trackage In and Around Macomb

The MI&L operated trains into Macomb in four different manners during its history. In addition, there was the original design for how the railroad was going to go through town, but which was never built. The original concept was for the railroad to come into town from the south up Johnson Street, turn east onto Jackson Street for two blocks until it reached Courthouse Square, turn north onto Lafayette Street for another two blocks, then turn east again and terminate along the CB&Q near Randolph Street at that railroad's depot. None of the trackage east of Johnson Street was ever built. What was built was a straight north-south line along Johnson which interchanged with the Burlington just south of the corner of Johnson and Calhoun Streets. This was the first operating arrangement for the railroad, and it lasted only a year, until December 30, 1904. At that time, homeowners along North Johnson Street were able to force the removal of the tracks on Johnson Street north of Jackson Street, and the railroad was cut back to the south side of the intersection of Johnson and Jackson Streets. During late 1904, the west side belt line was built as a means of restoring the railroad's interchange with the Burlington. This line began at the Macomb Yards, south of Grant and Johnson Streets, and across the street from the fairgrounds grandstands, and angled northwest to a meeting with the CB&Q at the West Sewerpipe Works on West Piper Street. This belt line was completed at the end of 1904, at the same time as the severing of the connection at North Johnson Street.[1]

This inaugurated the second operating arrangement for the line, which lasted until June 1908. Freight trains used the belt line on the west side, while passenger trains proceeded up Johnson Street to the depot at Johnson and Jackson Streets. When all M&WI trackage within the Macomb city limits was ordered removed in 1908, the third operating arrangement was temporarily put in place. Freight trains continued using the west side belt line, but passenger runs were cut short at the Macomb Yards, where passengers had to disembark and walk or take drays into downtown. This did not last too long, though, as in December 1909, an agreement was reached with the CB&Q, allowing M&WI passenger trains to proceed up the belt line and along the Burlington from the West Sewerpipe Works interchange into downtown Macomb. This fourth operating arrangement lasted until the sale to the wrecking company occurred in

January 1912. After the MI&L restarted operations in 1914, it again terminated passenger runs at the Macomb yards for a time, but by March 1915, it had again signed an agreement with the CB&Q to allow passenger trains to enter town from the west along the Burlington's tracks. This arrangement lasted until the service suspension in May 1928. After service resumed in

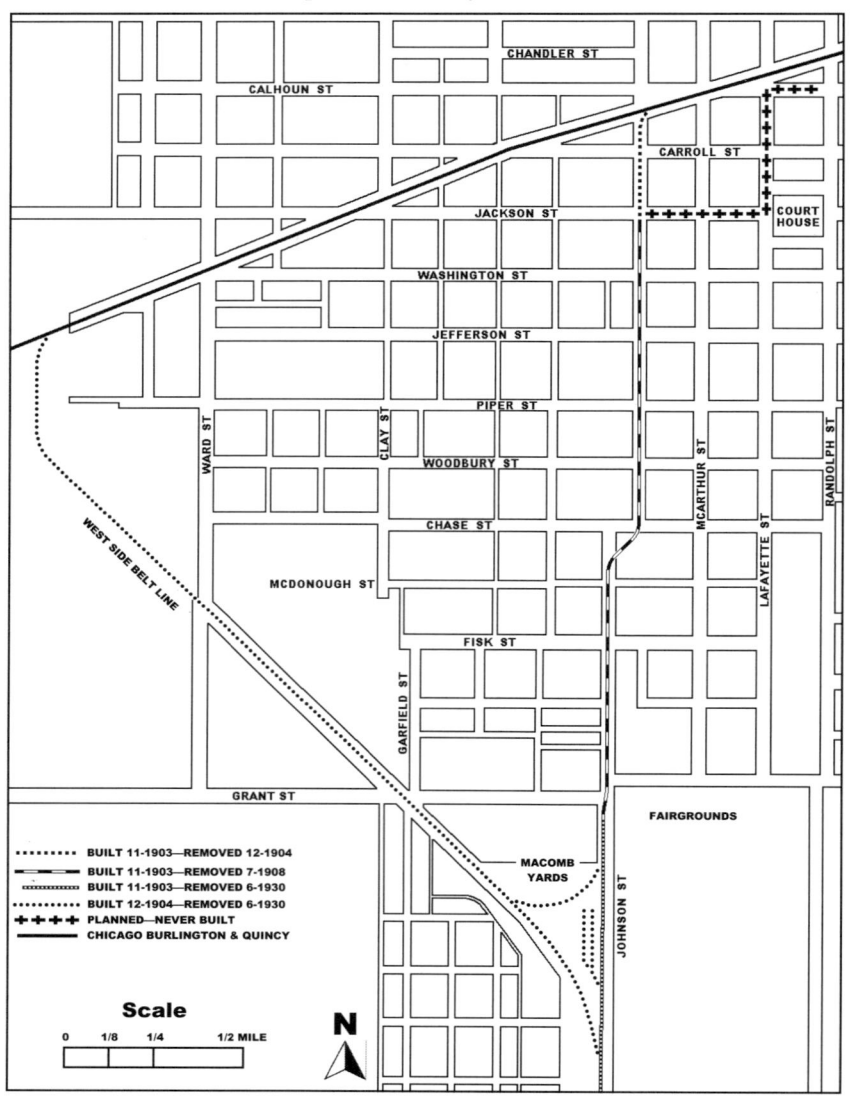

This map shows the routings of the railroad through Macomb. Trackage on Johnson Street was cut back to Jackson Street in 1904 and back to the edge of town in 1908. The West Side Belt Line was built in late 1904. Frank G. Hicks map.

August 1928, the railroad reverted to ending passenger service at the Macomb Yards.[2]

Trackage Between Macomb and Industry

The Macomb Yards, just south of St. Francis Hospital on Macomb's south side, were the primary storage and maintenance facilities for the railroad after they were built in late 1904. There was a wye, for turning engines, at the location surrounding the Yards. (The facilities will be described in the structures section.) From there, the railroad proceeded south along Rural Route 6, later the St. Francis Blacktop, running right along the west side of the road until it crossed the road a mile south of 500N and headed straight east into Industry along the north side of 400N. There were three major bridges between Macomb and Industry: at Troublesome Creek, at Camp Creek, and at Grindstone Creek. There were also three sidings, better known as switches, all of which were stops on the timetable. Not much is known about these switches. It is thought that all of them featured stockyards, but it is not known what other facilities, like waiting shelters or elevators, they included. It is not even known which side of the railroad main they were on, though the west side is most likely. Henderson Switch was the northernmost, located just north of Troublesome Creek at about 950N. Andrews Switch was located at about 600N. Kirkpatrick Switch was originally located at the curve south of Beaumont Road, but it was moved about half a mile north, to a point just north of Beaumont Road in May 1914.[3]

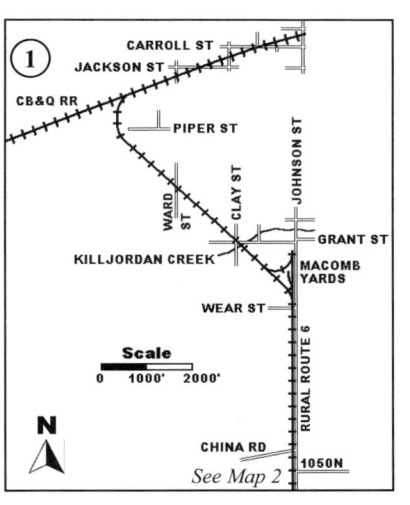

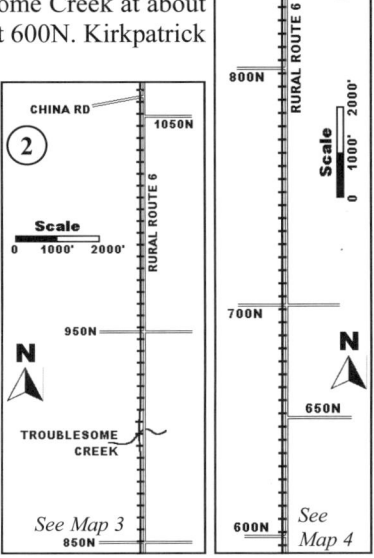

Trackage in Industry

The railroad entered Industry from the northwest along a curving alignment south of the current Route 67. The trackage around the Industry depot changed over time. Originally there was a short side track north of the depot leading to a stockyard, while later a longer passing siding was built that stretched nearly to First Street. The railroad continued south-southeast, crossing through the intersection of First and Hickory Streets before curving

TRACK AND STRUCTURES

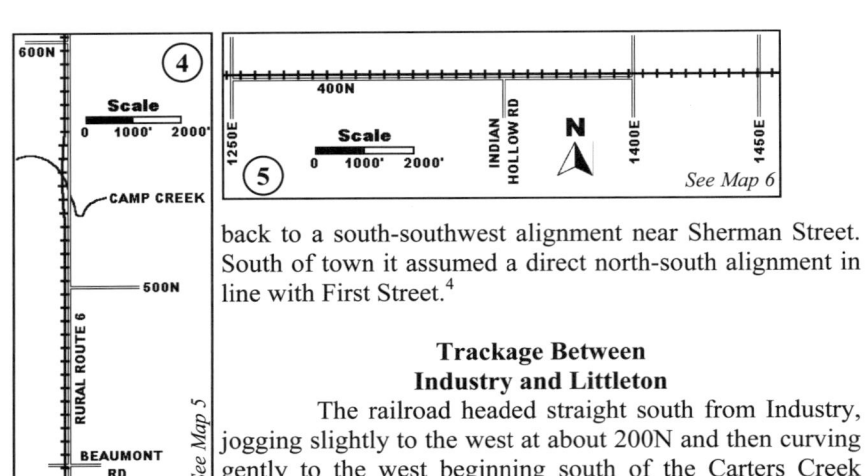

back to a south-southwest alignment near Sherman Street. South of town it assumed a direct north-south alignment in line with First Street.[4]

Trackage Between Industry and Littleton

The railroad headed straight south from Industry, jogging slightly to the west at about 200N and then curving gently to the west beginning south of the Carters Creek crossing. This was the only major bridge between Industry and Littleton, though there were a number of small bridges over minor streams. The railroad track crossed Ina Road heading southwest/northeast and turned to parallel that road along its southern edge. Runkle Switch, the only intermediate timetable location between Industry and Littleton, was located here. As with the other three switches, nothing concrete is known about the track layout at this location. This was the southern terminus of MI&L operations from February 8 to April 29, 1914, when the rails torn up by Chicago House Wrecking were relaid all the way into Littleton. The railroad turned straight south from Ina Road after about a thousand feet, assuming a north-south direction aligned with Main Street north of Littleton.[5]

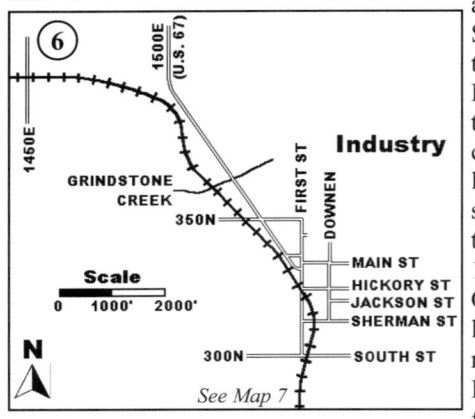

Trackage in Littleton

The railroad proceeded through Littleton on a straight north-south alignment, except for a slight bow to the east to accommodate the grade and culvert over Sugar Creek just north of downtown. The railroad extended south of Broadway for about 2,000 feet before terminating, and at this location there was a wye track which extended out to the west side of the main line. There were also one or two sidings just south of the depot, which was located on the southeast corner of the railroad's Broadway crossing.[6]

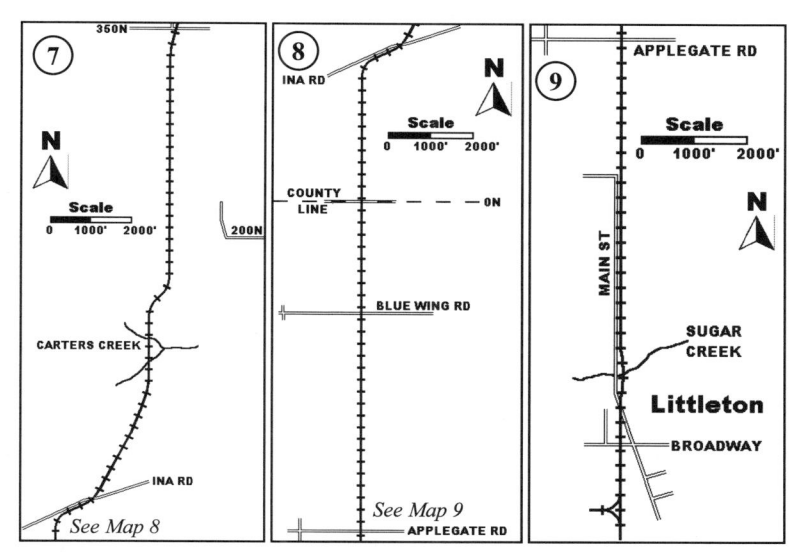

This series of maps of the railroad was drawn by the author using original US Geological Survey maps as a guide. These are route maps only and omit some detail such as sidings (switches), depots and wayside structures.

Structures in Macomb

The original depot for the M&WI was located in the front room of a blacksmith shop on the southeast corner of Jackson and Johnson Streets in Macomb. This depot was used until trackage within the city was removed in June 1908. During the period passenger service was cut back to Macomb Yards, no depot was used and tickets were sold only on the train. When the arrangement with the Burlington was first made, M&WI trains came into Macomb over the Burlington but did not use that railroad's station. Later, when the MI&L negotiated a new contract, the CB&Q depot was utilized as the Macomb depot and the Burlington station agent was paid partially by the MI&L. Sometime after the MI&L restored service into downtown Macomb over the CB&Q, it purchased a small brick building formerly used as a monument company for use as its depot. This building was located just northwest of the Burlington's Lafayette Street crossing. There were a couple of buildings at the Macomb Yards site along Johnson Street south of Grant Street. There was a two-stall engine house that was built in late 1904 and then burned down on December 31 of that year. It was rebuilt soon afterwards. There was also a water tower and a handcar storage house on this site. There was only one bridge in the Macomb area, a 400 foot long trestle built as part of the west belt line construction project in 1904 that crossed Killjordan Creek, and the low ground flanking Grant Street in the area of what is now Patton Park.[7]

Structures in Industry

The best-documented of any of the MI&L structures is the Industry depot, of which a number of photos exist. It was a small wooden frame structure located east of the tracks on the west side of town, 650 feet northwest of the elevator. Just south of the depot on the west side of the tracks was a water tower, with a small handcar shed located just south of the water tower. These structures were all built in 1904. The elevator, which was located further south, near First Street, was built in 1908, but was not actually owned by the railroad. There was also a small bridge on the northwest side of Industry which crossed Grindstone Creek.[8]

Structures in Littleton

Documentation of railroad structures in Littleton is somewhat sketchy. Located on the east side of the tracks on the south side of Broadway was a twenty-six by forty-foot depot built in the Pagoda style. This was either torn down or sold by the scrapping company in 1913, and company expense reports for 1914 include about $300 to either build a new depot or buy back the old one. The depot survived the railroad by half a century, but was destroyed by the 1981 tornado that devastated Littleton. The Littleton elevator is thought to have been located on the west side of the tracks north of Broadway Street on the approximate site of the current elevator. There was also a water tower located on the west side of the tracks just south of the depot. Further south, located alongside the wye near the southern terminus of the railroad, was the Littleton mine superstructure. This extended over the tracks and included an

This photo, probably taken around 1910, looks southeast at Industry. The depot is in the left foreground with the elevator (straight down the tracks) and water tower (to the right) beyond it. WIU Special Collections.

elevator apparatus which was designed to dump ore directly into railroad hopper cars. This structure was built in 1905, but it is unknown how long it lasted. The sale of mine property in 1918 may have included this site. Littleton facilities also included a stockyard, and in later years, a lumber yard, but their locations are uncertain. There was also a bridge on the near north side of Littleton which crossed Sugar Creek. In 1921 the bridge was replaced by a large culvert, which still exists.[9]

Structures Between the Towns

Except for bridges, little is known of the railroad structures located between the towns, other than that they were few and far between. Latter-day anecdotal evidence suggests that the facilities at Kirkpatrick Switch in the MI&L years included an elevator, stockyards, and a waiting shelter, built out of the body of an old passenger car, most likely car number 1 or car number 2. There may have also been an elevator and a stockyard located at Runkle Switch near the county line. Bridges included those over Troublesome Creek, at about 900N, Camp Creek, near 600N, Carters Creek, near Ina Road, and a few small bridges, culverts and overpasses. The Camp Creek bridge was the largest on the line. Thirty feet high and originally 340 feet long, though later shortened in length, it was a never-ending headache for the M&WI. It constantly needed repairs and the bridge and its approaches were especially susceptible to erosion from high water and rain. After the MI&L took over, the bridge was improved and was evidently less of a problem in later years.[10]

The only surviving photo of the Littleton depot is this shot, taken looking south with Broadway in the foreground. WIU Special Collections.

Appendix B
Rolling Stock

STEAM LOCOMOTIVES

No.	Type	Builder	Acquired	Former owner	Note*
1	0-4-4T	Baldwin	11/1903	Chic. Union Transfer 51	A
1	4-4-0	?	c1904-5?	?	B
2	4-4-0	?	c1905-6	?	C
4	4-4-0	?	c1907?	?	D
5	2-6-0	Davenport	4/1914	(new)	E
6	4-4-0	Pittsburgh	3/1915	Vandalia RR 302	F

INTERNAL COMBUSTION LOCOMOTIVES

No.	Type	Builder	Acquired	Note*
(none)	6-wheel boxcab	?	1903	G

PASSENGER CARS

No.	Type	Builder	Acquired	Note*
1	interurban/combine	St. Louis	1903	H
2	streetcar/coach	St. Louis	1904	I
4	combine	?	1908	J
?	combine	?	1920	K

FREIGHT CARS

Type	Quantity	Known Nos.	Note*
Boxcars	3	9, 101	L
Flatcars	5	102	M
Coal cars	1	?	N

MAINTENANCE-OF-WAY EQUIPMENT

Type	Quantity	Note*
Handcars	3	P
Push cars	2	P
Iron cars	1	P

*NOTES

A. The first locomotive 1 was built by Baldwin (serial #12990) as Chicago & South Side Rapid Transit 26 in October 1892. It was a Vauclain compound Forney type designed for rapid transit service. It ran on the Chicago elevated until it was sold in 1898 to Chicago Union Transfer, where it became their 51 and was assigned to Clearing Yard. It arrived in Macomb on November 22, 1903. The M&WI rebuilt it somewhat and used it in freight and passenger service during 1904.[1] It was sold off at some point, but exactly

Engine 1 (I) and coach 2 at Littleton during 1904, before the engine had even been painted for M&WI. This photo revealed the locomotive's former owner, C.U.T.Ry. L-R: Fireman James Ira Hodges, Engineer Tom Hendrickson, Conductor Roy Sullivan and Wheeler Wells. WIU Special Collections.

when and to whom is not known.

B. Little is known of the second locomotive 1. The only solid evidence of its existence is a photo of it in front of the Darius Runkle house, probably around 1905 (see photo on page 30). The M&WI purchased a 4-4-0 type locomotive on December 31, 1904, from the Chicago & North Western. The engine purchased, C&NW 467, was a Class E-4 engine built by Grant in 1882.[2] This was apparently the first large steam engine bought by the M&WI, and it is possible, but not certain, that this was M&WI 1. This may have been the engine listed in a 1913 valuation report as being stored unserviceable.

C. Engine 2 was used in passenger service around 1905 and 1906. The exact date it was acquired is unknown, and nothing is known of its past. It's possible, but unlikely, that this was ex-C&NW 467. This was the engine involved in the January 26, 1907, wreck in Industry. It was apparently not rebuilt after this derailment but rather was scrapped.[3] (See photo on front cover.)

D. Engine 4 was another 4-4-0 bought used from an unknown source at an unknown date. It is known that as of 1912, this was the only operational engine (another one, possibly engine number 1, was stored unserviceable at that time), and that it was the only motive power in use on the M&WI until the MI&L purchased engine 5 in April 1914. At that time, engine 4 was already badly worn out, and when engine 6 was bought in March 1915, this locomotive was scrapped.[4] (See photo on page 25.)

E. This locomotive was the only steam engine ever bought new by the "Little Road." It was a 2-6-0 "Mogul" designed for light branch or short line service. It was built by Davenport Locomotive Works, serial number 1478. It went through overhauls in 1920 at the CB&Q Aurora Shops, and in 1925 at Davenport. It is thought to have been in use from its date of construction until the last operation of the MI&L in early 1930. This was likely the last engine to operate on the line.[5] (See photo on page 45.)

F. The last locomotive ever bought by the MI&L was this one, a heavy 4-4-0 built by Pittsburgh Locomotive Works, serial number 694, in January 1884. It was classified a D-22 type by the Pennsylvania Railroad. Originally St. Louis Vandalia & Terre Haute 182, in June 1899, it became Terre Haute & Logansport 302, and later in 1905 it became Vandalia Railroad 302. The MI&L fitted it with a new boiler in 1917 and it was overhauled by Davenport Locomotive Works in 1922. It is believed that this locomotive was sold for scrap in 1928.[6] (See photo on page 47.)

G. The most unique piece of equipment to run on the railroad was this six-wheel box-cab gas-electric locomotive, delivered in late December 1903. Among the earliest internal combustion engines ever to have been put into service, its builder is unknown. Too far ahead of its time, it was severely

Combine 1 was brand new when this picture was taken in December 1903. Posing in front of it, left to right, are Roy Sullivan, "Happy Hooligan" Roy Ransom, James Ira Hodges, and Clarence Vial. WIU Special Collections.

underpowered and was of limited use. It was destroyed in the engine house fire on December 31, 1904.[7] (See photo on page 11.)

H. This car is well documented. It was built by the St. Louis Car Company, apparently on stock order 410A (the "A" meaning it was constructed in the old Laclede shops), and delivered new to the M&WI on December 16, 1903. Its design was that of a lightweight interurban. The vestibules were enclosed and the car was designed to be electrified. It even came with roof boards for supporting the trolley poles. It was painted Tuscan red, like all M&WI passenger equipment, and seated forty-four people. It apparently had no air brake equipment whatsoever. It was used for several years before being superseded by combine 4, but may have survived until 1913.[8]

I. The second passenger car bought by the M&WI was also built by St. Louis, this time on order 427. Ordered on November 13, 1903, it was delivered on February 25, 1904. It was a "Robertson" style semi-convertible car, designed as an electric streetcar, but fitted with couplers. The body was thirty-four feet long, the car seated forty-eight and it had St. Louis 23A trucks. Like car number 1, it was designed to be electrified later. Its body was not built for buffering forces associated with train operation, and it may not have lasted more than a few years before being retired. Either this car or car 1 was likely scrapped and placed at Kirkpatrick Switch for use as a waiting shelter sometime during the early MI&L years.[9] (See photo on page 21.)

J. Photographic evidence of the passenger cars used later in the railroad's life is sketchy, but documentary evidence is better. Sales receipts prove that a combine, almost certainly secondhand, was bought in late 1908 from the Georgia Car Company of Atlanta for $1,500 and lettered M&WI 4. It is thought that this may be the batten-board-sided car shown in the photo of engine 4 at Industry (see page 25) but that is not absolutely certain. This car apparently survived through the MI&L years, and was likely one of the two sold to Frank Haines for use as hog sheds when the railroad was scrapped in 1930.[10]

K. No photos exist of the last passenger car acquired by the MI&L, and its number on the "Little Road" is not even known. Documentary and newspaper evidence proves that in April 1920, a used fifty-four foot long combine

The 1903 gas-electric locomotive, "the motor," is shown here pulling coach 2 southbound at Industry during 1904. WIU Special Collections.

was bought for $2,700. It had formerly been Beaver Penrose & Northern 50. It is almost certain that this was one of the two cars sold to Frank Haines in 1930 for use as hog sheds.[11]

L. Little is known of the freight cars used by the railroad. The only available evidence comes from photographs and from valuations made at various times, which only list car totals. The 1913 valuations list three boxcars on the roster; by 1930 there were only two. A boxcar numbered 101 is shown in a 1904 photo in Macomb (see page 11), while a boxcar number 9 was among the equipment damaged in the 1907 wreck in Industry.

M. As with boxcars, little is known of the railroad's flatcar fleet. A photo dating to about 1904 shows a flatcar numbered 102 (see page 20). The 1913 valuations list four flatcars on the roster, and by the time the freight cars were all scrapped in 1930 there were five.

N. The definition of a "coal car" is uncertain. It may refer to the wood-sided gondola loaded with coal or ore which is shown in the photos of the 1907 wreck at Industry. The 1913 valuation lists this car, but it is missing from the 1930 list of scrapped freight cars.

P. Handcars, push cars, and iron cars were all lightweight equipment used in track maintenance that could be lifted on or off the tracks by a small group of men. Handcars were propelled by manpower, while push cars had no means of propulsion, but could be pushed by hand or pulled by a handcar. The purpose of iron cars was apparently to haul rail.[12]

ROSTER QUESTIONS

Several major questions about the rolling stock roster of the MI&L remain unanswered.

Where did the gas-electric locomotive come from? While ultimately unsuccessful, this engine was revolutionary for its time, yet there is virtually no record of who might have built it, nor was there any serious media coverage at the time of its construction.

What happened to the number "3"? Strangely enough, it appears that the M&WI skipped the number "3" in its numbering of both locomotives and passenger cars. It is possible that evidence of locomotive number 3 and passenger car number 3 simply hasn't been uncovered yet, but documentary evidence suggests these numbers simply weren't used. But why not?

Where did the M&WI get its 4-4-0s? There are records indicating that the M&WI bought its first 4-4-0 steam locomotive from the Chicago & North Western in 1904, but the origins of the other two engines of the same type which it bought secondhand are a mystery.

How did the railroad number its freight cars? Very early photos show freight cars numbered in the low 100 series, but a picture of the 1907 Industry wreck clearly shows a boxcar numbered 9. Did the freight car numbering scheme change at some point? Why?

Appendix C
MI&L Annual Reports

A number of annual reports from the MI&L during the 1910s and 1920s have survived and provide a clue to how precarious the railroad's operation was during that time. As the last annual report known to survive is from 1924, the real decline of the road from 1925 to 1930 is not well documented.

Receipts

	Freight	Passenger	Mail	Miscel.[1]	Total
1915	13,726.55	10,029.75	835.76	4,656.81	29,248.87
1916	17,883.42	10,171.28	795.18	1,395.86	30,245.74
1917	16,328.49	8,441.25	780.75	1,434.51	26,885.00
1917[2]	*16,912.76*	*7,855.48*	*975.81*	*18,278.11*	*44,022.16*
1918	22,776.00	8,277.71	822.03	20,516.50	52,392.24
1919	25,847.87	10,474.25	937.39	26,192.57	63,452.08
1920	20,511.61	10,804.72	1,420.86	28,833.38	61,570.57
1921	26,288.32	9,134.68	1,249.45	21,292.86	57,965.31
1922	25,498.05	7,789.23	1,224.04	19,497.43	54,008.75
1923	22,909.51	6,575.22	1,439.24	16,336.18	47,260.15
1924	25,047.70	6,050.46	1,333.36	27,405.62[3]	5,9832.14

1. This includes real estate rent, war tax (1917-1921 only), in 1918 includes the sale of mine property, and from 1918 on, includes advances (payments for the CB&Q), bills received and bills payable.
2. In 1918 the end of the fiscal year was changed from September 30 to December 31. The first 1917 line shows figures for the year ending September 30; the second line for the year ending December 31st. Also, prior to the 1918 (and the latter 1917) accounting, advances (CB&Q fees collected by the MI&L and forwarded), bills received and bills payable are not included.
3. This figure includes $6,000 of borrowed money.

Expenditures

	Operations	Maint.[4]	Terminal[5]	Miscel.[6]	Total
1915	10,177.52	3,742.10	1,866.14	12,252.77	28.038.53
1916	11,883.89	5,201.73	2,441.37	9,331.50	28,858.49
1917	11,668.03	9,191.65	2,425.55	8,273.91	31,549.14
1917[1]	*12,506.80*	*8,678.41*	*2,398.25*	*22,135.11*	*45,718.57*
1918	15,277.76	7,967.26	2,223.26	26,336.72	51,805.00
1919	14,379.75	14,556.48	2,718.93	32,240.31	63,895.47
1920	14,435.33	10,069.58		38,611.44[7]	63,116.02
1921	15,102.74	11,745.82		30,243.84	57,092.40
1922	14,212.46	12,294.15		27,591.62	54,098.23
1923	13,960.74	9,196.68		23,322.67	46,480.09
1924	13,157.51	14,276.31		33,621.31	61,055.18

4. Until 1919 this includes only road maintenance, while equipment and structures maintenance is included under "miscel" [sic]. From 1920 on, structures maintenance is lumped in with road maintenance.
5. Terminal fees, charged by the CB&Q for interchanging equipment, are broken out through 1919. After 1920, they are folded into one of the other categories, but that category is not specified in the reports.
6. This includes "miscellaneous operating charges," taxes, notes, and interest, war tax (1918-1921 only), and after 1917, includes advances (payments to the CB&Q).
7. Includes a $3,500 deposit made to the CB&Q for engine repairs and $2,700 for the purchase of new equipment, a combine.

Profit/Loss Figures

	Balance at end of fiscal year	Net Profit
1915	737.40	1,210.34
1916	2,124.65	1,387.25
1917	1,020.88	-1,103.77
1917[1]	*1,187.31*	n/a
1918	1,774.55	587.24
1919	1,331.16	-443.39
1920	-214.29	-1,545.45
1921	658.62	872.91
1922	569.14	-89.48
1923	1,149.20	780.06
1924	-68.84	-1,218.04

Freight Carriage Figures (in cars) [8]

	Grain cars	Stock cars	Merchandise[9]	Miscel.	Total
1915	189	222	535 (1124)	204	1,150
1916	211	273	(1378)	289	773[10]
1917	165	305	(1500)	314	784[10]
1917[1]	*252*	*268*	*303*	*320*	*1,143*
1918	275	393	284	382	1,334
1919	259	381	365	415	1,356[11]
1920	109	394	362	268	1,133
1921	175	400	326	182	1,083
1922	176	353	320	175	1,024
1923	141	372	258	183	954
1924	141	298	221	309	969

8. Figures for number of passengers carried are only available for 1916 (23,400) and 1917 (21,094).
9. Numbers in parentheses indicate total tons of less-than-carload merchandise carried.
10. Does not include cars of merchandise.
11. This figure is from the original report but doesn't come close to balancing; the source of the discrepancy is unknown.

Capital projects highlighted in surviving annual reports
Paraphrased from the original documents

1916
Placement of 7,718 cedar ties; ballasting and raising of 20,000 feet of track with cinders and heavy refuse from the Macomb Sewer Pipe Company and West Pottery; repairs to bridges over Troublesome, Grindstone, Carter, Saw Mill, Payne, and Camp Creeks; filling in sixty-nine feet of the south end of Camp Creek bridge and timbers removed; establishment of a lumber yard at Littleton.

1917
Placement of 5,434 cedar and 1,435 oak ties; purchase of a new boiler for engine 6 at a cost of $5,600.

1918
Placement of 2,555 cedar and 170 oak ties; replacement of several broken culverts and box culverts with boiler shells bought from their original owners.

1919
Placement of 3,953 ties; engine 5 will have to go through a general overhaul in spring 1920; a new coach is badly needed.

1921
Placement of 3,219 ties; new engine pit installed at the Macomb shop; boiler-

iron culvert installed at Finch crossing in Industry; new eight by nine fifty-foot culvert constructed at Winter Creek to replace former pile bridge; replacement of Gamage underpass with grade crossing.

1922
Placement of 4,177 ties; engine 6 put through Davenport Locomotive Works: engine tripped and dismantled, flues removed and overhauled, and new and larger tank cistern made, with a total cost, including new tender, of $4,300.

1924
Placement of 4,566 ties; repairs made to the Payne bridge; concrete box put in at Gamage cattle pass in Macomb; new stock chutes at Kirkpatrick switch and at Littleton; Littleton stock yard fences repaired.

End Notes

Chapter 1

1. Dr. Newton Bateman and Paul Shelby, *The Historical Encyclopedia of Illinois and History of McDonough County* (Chicago: Munsell Publishing, 1907): 617-618. The land encompassing Illinois County was known in its French days as Illinois *Country*.
2. James A. Edstrom, "Maps of Illinois Population and Newspaper History," *Harper College*, <http://www.harpercollege.edu/~jedstrom/maptableofcontents.htm> (10 May, 2005); Bateman and Shelby, 622-624; *Macomb Daily Journal*, 18 September 1914
3. Bateman and Shelby, 671-672, 678.
4. Ibid, 658, 678.
5. Schuyler County Jail Museum, *Schuyler County: Illinois History* (Dallas: Taylor Publishing, 1983): 6-7, 126
6. Albert J. Perry, *History of Knox County: Its Cities, Towns and People, Vol. I* (Chicago: S.J. Clarke Publishing, 1912): 591-592, 594
7. Ibid, 594-596, 598.
8. Ibid, 593-596, 598.
9. Bateman and Shelby, 681-682.
10. Ibid, 682-683; Alex Holmes, *History and Reminiscences of Alex Holmes* (Decorah, Iowa: Anundsen Publishing, 1987): 87-88.
11. Perry, 598; Edstrom; Bateman and Shelby, 676-679, 683.
12. G. Woodworth Colton, *Railroad Map of Illinois* (New York: G. Woodworth Colton, 1861), map; Bateman and Shelby, 683; Illinois Railroad and Warehouse Commission, *Annual Report for the Year Ending Nov. 30, 1872* (Springfield: State Journal Steam Print, 1873), 442-443.
13. *Macomb Daily Journal*, 1 March 1895, 23 November 1895
14. Ibid, 1 March 1895, 1 June 1895, 10 June 1895, 7 August 1895
15. Bateman and Shelby, 844-845.
16. 78th Illinois Infantry, *Regimental History: Adjutant General's Report*, quoted in Linda Lee, *78th Illinois Regimental History: Adjutant General's Report* <http://www.rootsweb.com/~ilcivilw/history/078.htm> (10 May 2005); Mark M. Boatner III, *The Civil War Dictionary* (New York: McKay Books, 1988): 151-152.
17. 78th Illinois Infantry, *Regimental History: Adjutant General's Report*; Bateman and Shelby, 845-846.
18. Bateman and Shelby, 846; John E. Hallwas, *Macomb: A Pictorial History* (G. Bradley Publishing, 1990): 80, 101.
19. *Macomb Daily Journal*, 1 June 1895, 10 June 1895, 7 August 1895
20. Ibid, 7 August 1895, 27 August 1895, 30 August 1895, 9 September 1895 (reprinted from the *St. Louis Chronicle*)
21. Ibid, 23 November 1895, 20 December 1895
22. Ibid, 20 December 1895, 1 April 1896, 27 April 1896, 16 June 1896, 16 June 1896 (reprinted from the *Lewistown News*), 17 November 1896

Chapter 2

1. Dr. Newton Bateman and Paul Shelby, *The Historical Encyclopedia of Illinois and History of McDonough County* (Chicago: Munsell Publishing, 1907): 855-856.
2. *Macomb Daily Journal*, 11 November 1901, 15 November 1901, 13 December 1901
3. Ibid, 12 November 1901, 13 November 1901, 15 November 1901, 26 November 1901
4. Ibid, 11 January 1902, 28 January 1902
5. Ibid, 16 May 1902, 28 June 1902, 12 July 1902, 22 August 1902, 1 October 1902, 3 October 1902
6. Ibid, 16 October 1902
7. Ibid, 24 October 1902, 13 November 1902, 20 November 1902, 15 December 1902
8. Ibid, 20 November 1902, 24 November 1902
9. Ibid, 30 January 1903, 13 February 1903, 28 March 1903
10. Ibid, 13 March 1903, 1 May 1903, 8 May 1903, 6 July 1903 (reprinted from the *Industry Enterprise*)
11. Ibid, 22 June 1903, 29 June 1903
12. Ibid, 14 August 1903, 15 August 1903, 17 August 1903, 28 August 1903, 25 September 1903. Most of the workers were locals and were paid wages of about $1.50 to $2.00 per day.
13. Ibid, 28 August 1903, 4 September 1903, 11 September 1903, 18 September 1903, 25 September 1903
14. Ibid, 2 October 1903, 16 October 1903, 28 October 1903 (reprinted from the *Rushville Citizen*)
15. Ibid, 11 November 1903, 1 December 1906
16. Ibid, 2 November 1903, 11 November 1903, 12 November 1903, 16 November 1903, 19 November 1903, 23 November 1903, 25 November 1903, 4 December 1903
17. Ibid, 2 December 1903, 18 December 1903 (reprinted from the *Industry Enterprise*)
18. Ibid, 17 December 1903, 23 December 1903, 26 December 1903; *Decision on Petition of Macomb and Western Illinois Rail Road Company*, McDonough County Board of Supervisors, 2 December 1901 Term.
19. *Macomb Daily Journal*, 23 December 1903, 26 December 1903, 29 December 1903, 30 December 1903
20. Ibid, 5 January 1904, 22 January 1904, 4 February 1904 (reprinted from the *Schuyler County Citizen*), 22 February 1904, 26 February 1904
21. Ibid, 18 March 1904, 1 April 1904, 8 April 1904
22. Ibid, 9 April 1904, 6 May 1904, 21 May 1904, 27 May 1904, 4 June 1904 (last four reprinted from the *Industry Enterprise*), 1 August 1904. The railroad used 60# rail and, according to the Illinois Railroad & Warehouse Commission's annual report for 1904, about two thirds of the route was earthen ballast while the remainder was either slag or cinder ballast.
23. Ibid, 5 January 1904, 22 April 1904, 29 April 1904 (last two reprinted from the

Industry Enterprise), 2 May 1904
24. Ibid, 2 May 1904, 1 August 1904
25. Ibid, 9 August 1904, 11 October 1904
26. Ibid, 9 August 1904, 11 October 1904, 13 October 1904
27. Ibid, 21 May 1904, 1 August 1904 (reprinted from the *Industry Enterprise*), 24 August 1904, 25 August 1904, 23 September 1904, 7 October 1904 (last two reprinted from the *Industry Enterprise*)
28. Ibid, 19 October 1904, 3 December 1904, 17 December 1904, 26 December 1904, 30 December 1904
29. Ibid, 2 January 1905; Joe Piersen, e-mail to the author, 26 August 2004
30. *Macomb Daily Journal*, 3 January 1905, 18 January 1905, 27 April 1905, 23 June 1906
31. Ibid, 2 September 1905, 2 January 1906, 23 June 1906, 28 September 1906, 30 November 1906
32. Ibid, 30 November 1906, 1 December 1906

Chapter 3

1. *Macomb Daily Journal*, 30 November 1906, 1 December 1906, 3 December 1906, 5 December 1906, 14 December 1906 (reprinted from the *Industry Enterprise*), 19 December 1906
2. Ibid, 26 January 1907, 28 January 1907
3. Ibid, 22 February 1907
4. Ibid, 31 May 1907, 1 June 1907, 10 June 1907, 2 June 1908. The original intended route to Lafayette Street (see map on page 60) would have been impossible for the M&WI's steam engines to traverse due to the sharp curves.
5. Ibid, 10 June 1907, 21 June 1907, 21 August 1907, 11 September 1907, 20 June 1908
6. Ibid, 18 June 1907, 27 June 1907, 28 June 1907, 1 July 1907, 2 July 1907, 3 July 1907
7. Ibid, 30 August 1907, 17 October 1907. It would appear the church had appealed the February ruling against it and the M&WI had decided to settle following the unfavorable judgment in Stuart's mandamus suit.
8. Ibid, 21 October 1907, 20 November 1907, 3 January 1908
9. Ibid, 2 June 1908, 8 June 1908, 25 June 1908 (reprinted from the *Blandinsville Star-Gazette*), 2 July 1908, 7 October 1908
10. Ibid, 16 June 1908, 18 June 1908, 2 July 1908, 6 July 1908, 14 July 1908, 5 August 1908, 7 October 1908
11. Ibid, 20 June 1908, 12 September 1908, 5 February 1909
12. Ibid, 20 June 1908, 7 October 1908, 27 October 1908, 28 October 1908, 5 February 1909
13. Ibid, 5 February 1909, 26 April 1909, 18 December 1909
14. Ibid, 6 January 1910, 4 October 1911, 18 September 1929; *Macomb Journal*, 27 February 1994
15. *Macomb Daily Journal*, 24 August 1910, 24 February 1911 (reprinted from the *Industry News*), 9 May 1911, 1 June 1911, 6 June 1911, 18 August 1911 (reprinted from the *Industry News*)

16. Ibid, 22 August 1911, 2 September 1911
17. Ibid, 21 September 1911, 4 October 1911, 3 January 1912, 23 January 1912

Chapter 4

1. *Macomb Daily Journal*, 31 January 1912, 1 February 1912
2. Ibid, 3 February 1912, 6 February 1912, 8 February 1912, 13 February 1912
3. Ibid, 13 February 1912
4. Ibid, 20 March 1912, 11 April 1912. $1.2 million in 1912 is equal to about $23.8 million in inflation-adjusted 2005 dollars.
5. Ibid, 20 March 1912, 22 March 1912, 23 March 1912, 25 March 1912, 26 March 1912, 2 April 1912, 11 April 1912
6. Ibid, 27 May 1912, 8 June 1912, 18 June 1912, 20 June 1912, 24 June 1912
7. Ibid, 26 June 1912, 26 July 1912, 13 August 1912, 28 August 1912, 16 September 1912
8. Ibid, 22 January 1913, 22 April 1913, 1 May 1913, 6 May 1913, 17 May 1913, 19 May 1913
9. Ibid, 19 May 1913, 20 May 1913, 23 May 1913, 26 May 1913
10. Ibid, 28 May 1913, 31 May 1913, 3 June 1913, 8 July 1913, 2 August 1913
11. Ibid, 8 August 1913, 13 August 1913, 15 August 1913
12. Ibid, 15 September 1913, 24 September 1913 (reprinted from the *Roseville Times-Citizen*), 24 September 1913, 26 September 1913, 1 October 1913
13. Ibid, 1 October 1913, 9 October 1913, 10 October 1913
14. Ibid, 9 October 1913, 11 October 1913, 13 October 1913, 20 October 1913
15. Ibid, 13 October 1913, 18 October 1913, 20 October 1913
16. Ibid, 25 October 1913
17. Ibid, 27 October 1913, 29 October 1913, 30 October 1913, 31 October 1913
18. Ibid, 31 October 1913, 1 November 1913, 3 November 1913
19. Ibid, 5 November 1913, 7 November 1913
20. Ibid, 11 November 1913, 14 November 1913, 22 November 1913, 25 November 1913
21. Ibid, 26 November 1913, 28 November 1913, 29 November 1913, 1 December 1913, 3 December 1913, 8 December 1913, 17 December 1913, 18 December 1913, 23 January 1914
22. Ibid, 23 December 1913, 24 December 1913, 27 December 1913 (reprinted from the *Industry News*), 27 December 1913, 30 December 1913, 31 December 1913. The $2,000 that Runkle and Clawson each pledged would translate to about $37,000 each in inflation-adjusted 2005 dollars.

Chapter 5

1. *Macomb Daily Journal*, 1 January 1914, 2 January 1914, 23 January 1914
2. Ibid, 1 January 1914, 2 January 1914
3. Ibid, 12 January 1914
4. Ibid, 13 January 1914, 14 January 1914, 20 January 1914, 23 January 1914 (reprinted from the *Industry News*), 24 January 1914, 30 January 1914, 3 February 1914, 4 February 1914

5. Ibid, 6 February 1914, 10 February 1914
6. Ibid, 23 January 1914, 10 February 1914, 26 February 1914, 27 February 1914
7. Ibid, 25 March 1914, 22 April 1914, 29 April 1914, 1 May 1914; Davenport Locomotive Company builder's photograph, Macomb Industry & Littleton Railway Company Papers 1901-1929, Western Illinois University Archives & Special Collections Department, Macomb, Illinois.
8. *Macomb Daily Journal*, 2 March 1915
9. Ibid, 11 March 1915, 12 March 1915, 17 March 1915, 18 March 1915; Bob Watson, e-mail to Les Beckman, 18 October 2004
10. *Industry Press*, 8 August 1918
11. Sales receipt, 23 April 1920, MI&L Papers; *Industry Press*, 28 May 1920; Correspondence between Macomb Industry & Littleton Railway and Railway Motor Car Company of America, 1920, MI&L Papers; *Macomb Daily Journal*, 11 January 1922, 10 January 1924, 23 January 1924
12. *Macomb Daily Journal*, 11 January 1922, 12 January 1923, 23 January 1924, 28 February 1925
13. Ibid, 28 February 1925, 3 September 1925
14. Ibid, 9 November 1925, 13 November 1925, 14 November 1925, 16 November 1925, 27 January 1926, 10 June 1926
15. Ibid, 10 June 1926, 25 January 1928, 10 May 1928, 21 May 1928, 8 June 1928, 9 June 1928, 23 June 1928, 5 February 1930; *Peoria Journal-Star*, 8 February 1930
16. *Macomb Daily Journal*, 23 June 1928
17. Ibid, 9 August 1928, 11 August 1928, 22 August 1928, 14 September 1928, 26 July 1929
18. Ibid, 10 July 1929, 26 July 1929, 1 August 1929
19. Ibid, 24 September 1929, 3 October 1929, 10 October 1929; *McDonough County News*, 24 October 1929 (reprinted from the *Rushville Times*)
20. *Macomb Daily Journal*, 25 October 1929, 17 January 1930, 5 February 1930, 31 March 1930
21. Ibid, 22 April 1930, 1 May 1930, 3 May 1930, 5 May 1930, 21 May 1930, 29 May 1930, 12 June 1930, 19 June 1930, 24 June 1930

Appendix A

1. *Macomb Daily Journal*, 15 April 1903, 11 November 1903, 12 November 1903, 2 May 1904, 1 August 1904, 9 August 1904, 3 December 1904, 6 December 1904, 30 December 1904; United States Geological Survey, *Illinois: Macomb Quadrangle* (Washington: United States Geological Survey, 1912), map.
2. *Macomb Daily Journal*, 1 August 1904, 2 June 1908, 3 June 1908, 8 June 1908, 18 December 1909, 6 February 1912, 27 February 1914, 29 April 1914, 2 March 1915, 2 August 1928
3. Ibid, 13 February 1903, 13 May 1903, 22 June 1903, 11 July 1903, 24 July 1903, 1 April 1904, 1 August 1904, 6 January 1912, 1 May 1914; Sanborn Map Company, *Macomb, Illinois* (New York: Sanborn Map Company, 1924), map, sheet 10; United States Geological Survey (1912), map; George A. Ogle & Company, Standard Atlas of McDonough County, Illinois (Chicago: George

A. Ogle & Company, 1913): 14.

4. United States Geological Survey (1912), map; Sanborn Map Company, *Industry, Illinois* (New York: Sanborn Map Company, 1928), map, sheet 1; Photograph of Industry depot, MI&L Papers.

5. United States Geological Survey (1912), map; *Macomb Daily Journal*, 23 January 1914, 27 February 1914, 29 April 1914. It should be pointed out that the location of Runkle Switch is not absolutely certain: the Runkle family owned vast tracts of land along both sides of the MI&L between Industry and Littleton. The 1912 USGS map shows several buildings adjoining the MI&L at Ina Road, and other circumstantial evidence suggests this was the location of Runkle Switch.

6. United States Geological Survey, Illinois: Rushville Quadrangle (Washington: United States Geological Survey, 1923), map; Photograph of Littleton depot, MI&L Papers; Microsoft Corporation, *Terraserver USA*, 11 April 1998, <http://terraserver.microsoft.com> (4 October 2005).

7. *Macomb Daily Journal*, 5 January 1904, 19 October 1904, 3 June 1908, 18 December 1909, 2 March 1915; Sanborn, *Macomb*, sheet 5. It is not known for certain that the depot at Jackson and Johnson Streets was used until 1908 but it is unlikely another one was built on the same site. There is also mention in the records of a bridge over Killjordan being built in July 1903, which may refer to the rebuilding of the Johnson Street bridge. The small brick building just north of the CB&Q on the east side of Lafayette Street in Macomb resembles the MI&L 1920s office and may in fact be that building, but at the time of this writing its heritage could not be definitively determined.

8. Photograph of Industry depot area, MI&L Papers; *Macomb Daily Journal*, 13 February 1903, 23 December 1903, 6 May 1904, 21 May 1904, 18 June 1904; Sanborn, *Industry*, sheet 2

9. *Macomb Daily Journal*, 22 February 1904, 24 October 1904, 2 September 1905, 2 January 1906, 26 September 1913; Photograph of Littleton depot, MI&L Papers; G.S. Rollett. "Stockholders Report for Year Ending Sept. 30th, 1916" (Macomb Industry & Littleton Railway Company, Industry, Illinois, 1916, mimeographed); Audit, Business Services & Audit Company, 22 January 1919, MI&L Papers. There is some confusion as to the name of what is nowadays Sugar Creek. Company records never mention Sugar Creek but the 1921 MI&L annual report does record construction of a "concrete culvert, size 8x9, 50 feet" to replace the bridge over "Winters Creek." It is thought that this sizeable culvert may in fact be the one currently still intact at Sugar Creek on the north side of Littleton, however it is just an assumption that Winters Creek and Sugar Creek are the same.

10. *Macomb Daily Journal*, 24 July 1903, 1 April 1904, 2 January 1914, 23 January 1914; Rollett (1916); United States Geological Survey (1912), map; *Macomb Sunday Journal*, 1986/10/12; information on the structures at Kirkpatrick Switch is from the reminiscences of Nellie Kirkpatrick Pollock, while the identity of the passenger car is conjecture. A structure apparently resembling a railroad waiting shelter remains (in 2005) near the site of the Runkle Switch but its heritage cannot be definitively determined.

Appendix B

1. Central Electric Railfans Association, *Chicago's Rapid Transit: Volume I* (Chicago: Central Electric Railfans Association, 1973): 2, 6; Photographs of M&WI locomotive 1 at Littleton and Industry, MI&L Papers; Macomb Daily Journal, 23 November 1903, 1 April 1904, 22 April 1904, 27 May 1904.
2. Joe Piersen, e-mail to the author, 26 August 2004
3. Photographs of 1907 Industry wreck, MI&L Papers; *Macomb Daily Journal*, 21 February 1907
4. *Macomb Daily Journal*, 2 January 1914, 12 March 1915; Audit, 22 January 1919, MI&L Papers. According to the newspaper article engine 4 was to be rebuilt, but the MI&L didn't really need it, and the audit report from four years later makes it clear the locomotive had been retired.
5. Davenport Locomotive Company builder's photograph, MI&L Papers; Invoice, Chicago Burlington & Quincy – Aurora Locomotive Shop, 22 November 1920, MI&L Papers. The assumption that this was the last operational locomotive is conjecture. On 11 August 1928 the Macomb Daily Journal claims that both of the railroad's engines (5 and 6) had been traded away for a better locomotive, but on 5 February 1930 Charles Flack released a statement mentioning, among other things, that the railroad was still using a locomotive bought in 1914. It seems likely that the newspaper was simply in error in its 1928 report, though aged engine 6 was quite possibly sold for scrap at that time. After the railroad was abandoned, its engine, almost certainly 5, was towed to Galesburg for rebuilding. What became of it after that is not known.
6. Bob Watson, e-mail to Les Beckman, 18 October 2004; A.C. Anders. "Annual Report of Receipts and Expenditures" (Macomb Industry & Littleton Railway Company, Industry, Illinois, 1922, mimeographed); G.S. Rollett. "Annual Report of the Macomb, Industry & Littleton Ry. Co." (Macomb Industry & Littleton Railway Company, Industry, Illinois, 1917, mimeographed); see the note above concerning engine number 5 for details on its disposition.
7. *Macomb Daily Journal*, 26 December 1903, 27 May 1904, 2 January 1905; Photographs of the M&WI box cab locomotive at Macomb, MI&L Papers.
8. Alan Lind, *From Horsecars to Streamliners: An Illustrated History of the St. Louis Car Company* (Park Forest: Transport History Press, 1978): 328; Dr. Harold Cox, e-mail to the author, 2 September 2004; *Macomb Daily Journal*, 17 December 1903; Photograph of M&WI combine 1 upon delivery, MI&L Papers. Information about this car's service life after about 1907 is conjecture; the only photo of combine #1 after 1904 is the picture of it with engine #1 in front of the Darius Runkle house north of Littleton. The 1913 valuation report (*Macomb Daily Journal*, 20 May 1913) lists three passenger cars, one of which must surely be the combine bought in 1908; one of the others is probably this car.
9. Lind, 330; Photograph of M&WI coach 2, MI&L Papers; *Macomb Daily Journal*, 26 February 1904. Speculation about the car's resistance to buffering forces is taken from photographic evidence and from the author's own experience with railway car construction. A *Macomb Sunday Journal* article from 12 October 1986 mentions a railway car body being used as a shelter at

Kirkpatrick switch; this may or may not have been this car.
10. Sale contract between MI&L and Georgia Car Company, 9 October 1908, MI&L Papers; *Macomb Daily Journal*, 24 June 1930. It's not certain that this car was one of the last two passenger cars owned by the railroad but it seems likely.
11. *Industry Press*, 28 May 1920; Sales receipt, 23 April 1920, MI&L Papers; *Macomb Daily Journal*, 24 June 1930. It's not certain this was one of the two cars sold in 1930 but since this was the line's newest car, it's quite likely.
12. *Macomb Daily Journal*, 20 May 1913, 19 June 1930, 24 June 1930; Audit, 22 January 1919, MI&L Papers.

Bibliography

Bateman, Dr. Newton and Paul Shelby. *The Historical Encyclopedia of Illinois and History of McDonough County*. Chicago: Munsell Publishing, 1907.

Boatner, Mark M. *The Civil War Dictionary*. New York: McKay Books, 1988.

Central Electric Railfans Association. *Chicago's Rapid Transit: Volume I*. Chicago: Central Electric Railfans Association, 1973.

Chrisinger, J.W. *Map of Macomb, Illinois*. Macomb: Macomb By-Stander, 1906, map.

Colton, G. Woodworth. *Railroad Map of Illinois*. New York: G. Woodworth Colton, 1861, map.

Decision on Petition of Macomb and Western Illinois Rail Road Company. McDonough County Board of Supervisors, 2 December 1901 Term.

Edstrom, James A., "Maps of Illinois Population and Newspaper History," *Harper College*, < http://www.harpercollege.edu/~jedstrom/maptableofcontents.htm > (10 May 2005).

George A. Ogle & Company. *Standard Atlas of McDonough County, Illinois*. Chicago: George A. Ogle & Company, 1913.

Hallwas, John E. *Macomb: A Pictorial History*. St. Louis: G. Bradley Publishing, 1990.

Hillery, Viletta, interview by the author, tape recording, Macomb, Illinois, 16 November 2004.

Holmes, Alex. *History and Reminiscences of Alex Holmes*. Macomb: By-Stander Press, 1923.

Illinois Railroad and Warehouse Commission. *Annual Report for the Year Ending Nov. 30, 1872*. Springfield: State Journal Steam Print, 1873.

_____. *Thirty-Fourth Annual Report*. Springfield: Illinois State Journal Company, 1905.

Industry Press, 8 August 1918, 28 May 1920.

Lind, Alan. *From Horsecars to Streamliners: An Illustrated History of the St. Louis Car Company*. Park Forest: Transport History Press, 1978.

Macomb Daily Journal, 1 March 1895-24 June 1930.

Macomb Industry & Littleton Railway Company Papers 1901-1929, Western Illinois University Archives & Special Collections Department, Macomb, Illinois.

Macomb Journal, 27 February 1994.

Macomb Sunday Journal, 12 October 1986.

McDonough County News, 24 October 1929.

Microsoft Corporation. *Terraserver USA*. 11 April 1998. <http://terraserver.microsoft.com> (4 October 2005).

Peoria Journal-Star, 8 February 1930.

Perry, Albert J. *History of Knox County: Its Cities, Towns and People, Volume I*. Chicago: S.J. Clarke Publishing, 1912.

Rand, McNally & Company. *Railroad Map of Illinois*. Chicago: Rand,

McNally & Company, 1898, map.

Sanborn Map Company. *Industry, Illinois*. New York: Sanborn Map Company, 1928, map.

_____. *Macomb, Illinois*. New York: Sanborn Map Company, 1924, map.

Schuyler County Jail Museum. *Schuyler County: Illinois History*. Dallas: Taylor Publishing, 1983.

Shadwick, G.W. *The History of McDonough County*. Moline, Illinois: Desaulniers, 1968.

United States Geological Survey. Illinois: Macomb Quadrangle. Washington: United States Geological Survey, 1912, map.

_____. Illinois: Rushville Quadrangle. Washington: United States Geological Survey, 1923, map.